EUROPEAN ECONOMIC INTEREST GROUPINGS

Commercial, legal and tax considerations

EUROPEAN ECONOMIC INTEREST GROUPINGS
Commercial, legal and tax considerations

Patrick Kelly BA
Ptnr, Laytons, Solicitors, Lincoln's Inn Fields, London

Rebecca Attree MA
Assistant Solicitor, Laytons, Solicitors, Lincoln's Inn Fields, London

Iain Muir BAcc (Hons) CA, ATII
Ptnr, tax division, Arthur Andersen & Co, Glasgow

Christopher Wales MA, PhD, ACA
Ptnr, tax division, Arthur Andersen & Co, London

Katarina Labaere Llc Jur, MA
European Affairs Consultant, Price Waterhouse Consultants SA, Brussels

Pamela Clark BA (Hons), ALA, MI Inf Sc
Head of Library and Information Services, SG Warburg & Co Ltd, London

Peter Van Duzer LLB
Solicitor, Jordans, London

JORDANS
1990

Published by
Jordan & Sons Ltd
21 St Thomas Street
Bristol BS1 6JS

British Library Cataloguing in Publication Data

European Economic Interest
Groupings: commercial, legal and tax considerations.
1. European Community countries.
European Economic Interest Groupings
I. Kelly, Patrick

ISBN 0 85308 154 9

Typeset by APS Typesetters, Salisbury
Printed by Bocardo Press, Didcot

PREFACE

With the explosion of interest in cross-border joint ventures in Europe and the rapidly increasing number of small and medium-sized enterprises becoming involved in international collaboration, the European Economic Interest Grouping (EEIG) provides an attractive and flexible vehicle for European co-operation. This book provides practical answers to the key questions which an organisation contemplating an EEIG needs to address:

What kinds of venture are EEIGs suitable for? What are the formation and other legal considerations? How will EEIGs be treated for tax purposes in the UK and EC? Who would be a suitable partner for collaboration?

A multi-disciplinary team of expert authors has evaluated the practical considerations involved in setting up and using this new form of business enterprise, examining it in detail from a number of crucial angles.

Peter Van Duzer, a solicitor at Jordan & Sons Ltd, has provided a succinct introduction outlining the main features of this new corporate joint venture vehicle.

Katarina Labaere, who is a manager at Price Waterhouse Consultants, EC Services in Brussels, responsible for assessing the impact of EC regulations and policy, has explained the ways in which EEIGs can be set to work and looked at examples of how European businesses are already making use of them.

Patrick Kelly, a solicitor and partner of Laytons, and Rebecca Attree, a solicitor with Laytons, have examined in detail all the legal considerations from a practical point of view answering many of the most important questions which anyone considering entering into an EEIG would need to address.

Iain Muir, a partner of Arthur Andersen & Co, and Christopher Wales, a tax consultant with the same firm, have conducted a penetrating critical analysis of the tax position of EEIGs both with respect to UK and European taxes.

Pamela Clark, who is head of library and information services at the merchant bank S G Warburg & Co Ltd, provides some very useful advice on how to go about locating suitable partners with whom to form an EEIG.

Viewed from these different angles, a clear profile of European Economic Interest Groupings emerges, enabling informed decisions to be taken as to how best to benefit from the new opportunities which EEIGs will open up for European business in the 1990s.

JORDANS
September 1990

CONTENTS

CHAPTER ONE
INTRODUCTION TO EEIGS

The International Context

We are all aware of the increasing internationalisation of businesses. This appears most obviously in major sectors such as the motor industry, but all commercial organisations should be aware that the international approach is not only increasing its influence in areas where it is already prevalent but is also spreading to smaller organisations and businesses which would not previously have felt its effects.

Within Europe we have a particular force driving us towards a more international approach, in the form of the commitment to create a single market by the end of 1992. This commitment is for an area without internal frontiers, to allow for the free movement of goods, services, capital and people. The thrust of this has resulted in an accelerating programme of proposals and measures leading towards an open market comprising some 323 million people. The prospect of this large international market appears to be concentrating many commercial minds on the possibilities of extending their activities into new markets in Europe, on how to face the likely increased competition from other businesses in Europe and on possible collaboration with other European businesses to further the activities of all parties both within and outside Europe.

In the past it has been relatively common for larger-scale businesses to enter into joint ventures with each other where their resources, skills and markets are complimentary to each other, for instance in the high technology sector. This has been less common among smaller organisations, but many medium-sized and smaller organisations are now recognising the need for a change of approach to take advantage of the wider international context in which they will operate and meet the challenges which this will offer.

It seems that although international joint venture activity has been increasing, the emphasis has shifted away from co-operation with a partner from within the EC towards co-operation with a non-EC partner. This may perhaps be as a result of those based outside the EC attempting to set up a business activity in Europe which they can use to trade within the larger European market which is coming into being. However, in the light of these changing market conditions, there seems to be no reason why businesses situated in Europe should not take advantage of the possibilities offered by joint venture activity to combine their resources, skills and knowledge more effectively for specific purposes. Such co-operation is likely to become increasingly necessary to enable smaller organisations to effectively compete. Specifically, European businesses will need to collaborate across borders inside the EC to compete both within the EC and beyond.

When considering co-operation with other organisations, questions to be addressed include the activities which the co-operation is to encompass, the form of structure to be used for such co-operation, the legal and taxation considerations and the identification of a suitable partner for collaboration. The form of structure may include a range of options such as an agency agreement or other contractual relationship, a partnership, the use of a jointly owned subsidiary, or even acquisition of another business or merger of the parties. One possible form of structure which has been available since 1 July 1989 has been the European Economic Interest Grouping (often referred to as 'EEIG' or 'Grouping'). Both businessmen and their professional advisers should be aware of this relatively recent addition to the armoury of structures available for international business co-operation and of where it may be appropriately used.

What is an EEIG?

An EEIG is a new form of business organisation created by a European Community Council Regulation which applies to all countries in the European Community. Thus, the EEIG is a common legal concept throughout all the Member States (although its actual name may vary). The purpose of its creation as a legal concept is to contribute to the achievement of effective co-operation by individuals and organisations carrying on commercial activities in different countries within the European Community.

Who can be its Members?

An EEIG must have a minimum of two Members having their central administration or their principal activities in different Member States of the European Community. It is therefore necessarily international in concept as it will need Members from at least two different EC countries, although a larger EEIG with more than two Members might well have some of its Members from the same country. The Members may be companies, firms, partnerships or other legal bodies of any type formed in accordance with the law of a Member State having their registered office and central adminsitration in a Member State and also natural persons who carry on business activities with their principal activities in a Member State. Therefore possible Members include a wide range, from companies, or other legal bodies (eg universities), to individual businessmen – so long as they are EC-based.

What can it Do?

When a Grouping is set up, its purpose must be to facilitate or develop the economic activities of its Members and to improve or increase the results of those activities. Its purpose is not to make profits for itself in isolation, but to enable its Members to improve their own results. Its activity must be related to the economic activities of its Members and must not be more than ancillary to these activities. It can thus be seen that an EEIG cannot be used for a new activity entirely unrelated to the existing businesses of its Members, nor can one of its Members only carry on activity through the EEIG – the Member must also have his own activities outside the EEIG. However these provisions should not be seen as unduly restrictive. It is clear, for instance, that EEIGs can make a profit and it appears that the word 'ancillary' can be interpreted in a fairly broad way. There are also certain other restrictions imposed on an EEIG with regard to exercising management or supervision over its Members, holding shares in its Members or employing more than 500 persons. As will be seen later, despite these restrictions, there are still a large number of areas and activities where an EEIG may usefully operate.

What Form does it Take?

An EEIG has the capacity, in its own name, to have rights and obligations, to make contracts or accomplish other legal acts, and to sue and be sued. Thus in layman's terms it will be able to interact with the outside world in very much the same way as an incorporated company, except that its Members have *unlimited* liability. It is formed by a contract between its Members which is then registered. The contract must include at least the name, address, objects and duration (which may be indefinite) of the EEIG and details of its Members. Beyond this, the contents of the contract between the Members are entirely flexible and can be designed as the Members wish. Following its completion, the contract and necessary forms must be registered at the appropriate Registry in the country in the EC in which the EEIG will have its official address. The EEIG will then come into existence.

Its Members will have unlimited joint and several liability. The decision-making bodies of the EEIG will be (a) its Members acting collectively who have ultimate authority, (b) its managers (who occupy a broadly similar position to that of directors of a company), and (c) any other decision-making body which the Members decide to add under the terms of the contract.

What are the Advantages of the EEIG?

EEIGs offer certain advantages over other types of business entity when a joint venture co-operation or amalgamation are proposed. It may be helpful to summarise some of them here. First, it has capacity to do things in its own name (like a company) combined with the flexibility of being almost entirely designed and regulated by an agreement between its Members (like a partnership). Secondly, it has a legal structure recognised in all Member States of the EC and which is relatively common throughout the EC, subject to minor differences in the implementing legislation of the Member States. Thirdly, it provides a flexible vehicle which does not require a fixed capital contribution. Members can contribute expertise, plant, capital, etc, as they may agree and this agreement may be varied at a later date as necessary. Its structure is also very flexible. Finally, it offers an effective way of co-operating with a foreign partner or partners without a loss of independence by the Members. It is effective in this way because it is constituted as a legal body, separate from its Members, with its own capacity to contract. It can therefore project its own identity when dealing with others in a manner which can (if appropriate) be quite separate from the identities of its Members and can follow this up by entering into contracts of a legal nature in its own name. This will offer advantages over a joint venture which merely proceeds under the terms of an agreement. In this way, an EEIG offers similar advantages to a jointly owned subsidiary. Both these options provide a legal body which stops short of actual merger or acquisition of the whole business. Alteration to the terms of the Agreement for the EEIG or even the dissolution of the EEIG will always be optional should it prove unsuccessful.

What are the Disadvantages of the EEIG?

First, unlimited joint and several liability of the Members for the debts of the Grouping. This may be unattractive to many businesses thinking of joining an EEIG. Under this principle, as it applies to EEIGs, a creditor may proceed against a Member of the EEIG for payment in respect of debts and other liabilities of the EEIG if the EEIG has been liquidated or has not made payment of a debt within a reasonable period in response to a request. In such a case the creditor might proceed against one Member for the full debt outstanding. It might be possible for each Member to negotiate suitable indemnities from the other parties and agree limits with the other parties regarding suitable indebtedness.

The second disadvantage is that the apparent flexibility of contributions and use of an EEIG may be curtailed when taxation considerations are fully considered.

Finally, restrictions on the activities may make an EEIG unsuitable for certain ventures (eg those in areas unconnected with the existing business of the Members).

Both the advantages and disadvantages of an EEIG should appear more clearly from the chapters which follow.

The Uses for an EEIG

Time will tell which activities prove to be the most popular area of operation for EEIGs, but it will generally take on a supporting and co-operative role for its Members. Possible areas are indicated in further detail in Chapter 2. However, typical areas where EEIGs could be applied are:.

1. Joint tendering for a major works project and co-ordination of the works project following acceptance of the tender.
2. Joint purchasing.
3. Joint distribution.
4. Joint marketing.
5. Joint research and development.
6. Joint manufacturing and/or assembly.

It is interesting to note that one group which has quickly taken advantage of the new form of business entity provided by the EEIG is firms of lawyers. Possibly because in the early stages they were the people most aware of the uses and advantages of this new form of business organisation. EEIGs have also been formed in other countries for joint research, promotion and purchasing. Diverse bodies are participating as Members of different EEIGs including (amongst others) the Crown Agents and management colleges. There are many other reasons for the formation of an EEIG apart from the obvious economic advantage. For the professions and service organisations, it may enable firms to offer a European-wide range of services for businessmen now operating in other countries. For manufacturing and other businesses it may enable them to present a European 'image' for marketing or other purposes. For organisations such as teaching institutions, museums, etc, it may enable a more effective exchange of information or pooling of resources.

The breadth of possible applications for EEIGs will become apparent as commercial organisations seek to apply them to their particular needs. These may range from very specialised uses to the general joint development and promotion of products or services. The co-operation may exist to bridge the gap between industry and research institutions such as universities, or it may constitute a relatively straightforward co-operation between two or more businesses. In many cases an EEIG may provide a vehicle for co-operation where the necessity to use less ideal structures had hampered collaboration in the past.

Legal and Taxation Considerations

The legal and taxation implications of the proposed venture will first have been considered when evaluating the suitability of an EEIG as opposed to other possible forms of commercial vehicle. Once it has been decided that an EEIG may be a possible commercial vehicle for a particular purpose, it will be necessary to consider the legal and tax implications again in more detail when drafting the Agreement for the operation of the EEIG. By way of very brief summary of the taxation considerations, the European Community Council Regulation provides that the profits or losses resulting from the activities of an EEIG shall be taxable only in the hands of its Members. Therefore for these purposes an EEIG is tax transparent. However, this leaves aside other taxation implications such as payroll taxes for staff of the EEIG, VAT and transfer duties. It also leaves aside possible capital gains taxes which may arise on the transfer of assets into or out of the EEIG.

Difficulties may arise in situations where an EEIG is involved in the payment or receipt of interest or royalties on a cross-border basis, where an EEIG is operating in non-EC countries, where capital gains are made, or on the transfer of property into and out of the EEIG. However, it should be emphasised that taxation problems are not peculiar to the EEIG and are likely to arise in any form of cross-border co-operation by businesses. It is essential to ensure that appropriate consideration is given to such matters when choosing the organisation to be used for international co-operation. The legal and taxation considerations are considered in more detail in Chapters 3 and 4.

Identifying a Prospective Partner

It is envisaged that the EEIG may provide opportunities to business organisations which would previously not have been involved in international joint ventures, as well as providing further possibilities for larger organisations already familiar with such matters. For the medium-sized and smaller business, guidance may be appropriate to find prospective partners for an EEIG, particularly where there are two prospective members who wish to find others to join them to make the project viable. Advances in information gathering and technology mean that the vital importance of finding the right partners for participation in the EEIG can now be a much more precise operation than many might believe. An informative study of this question is contained in Chapter 5.

If a business is seeking a partner in a particular industry, an international directory for that industry may provide helpful information for initial purposes. Beyond this, the use of electronic databases, in conjunction with appropriate software, will enable the selection of lists of appropriate partners in accordance with pre-set criteria fixed in accordance with the requirements which are sought in any prospective partner. These criteria might include geographical location, type of business activity, number of employees, etc. Other databases containing general information may also be of assistance. After this, if further information with regard to specific companies is required this may be possible to obtain either through an appropriate database or by making a search at the particular registry involved. Credit-rating services may also be used. Databases can be accessed to compare the financial performance of companies and gain other information. In summary, there is a great deal of information available and professional use of available databases and technology may produce a very detailed list of target partners. However, it must be recognised that, particularly for the smaller business, the search for suitable partners to fill a defined need may pose a major problem. Whilst the careful use of available data may reduce this problem it is unlikely altogether to eradicate it in circumstances where the partner sought is a small or unincorporated business.

The EEIG offers an additional form of commercial organisation which must be taken into account by those businesses involved in international co-operation and it presents exciting opportunities to the larger number of businesses only now starting to become involved in this area. The EEIG is not only something which businessmen must expect to deal with as an outsider, but also something which they should consider in relation to their own business as they plan to enter into the European and international arena.

CHAPTER TWO
PRACTICAL APPLICATIONS FOR EEIGS

Introduction

This chapter explores how business uses the European Economic Interest Grouping ('EEIG' or 'Grouping'), a form of enterprise designed to facilitate and develop cross-frontier co-operation in the European Community ('EC') between companies, institutions and/or individuals.

To begin with, the significance of this novel corporate entity is stressed from an EC perspective. There is a discussion of the practical and commercial implications of EEIGs followed by a case study of how and why one particular consortium of large corporations is using an EEIG. Numerous concrete examples of Groupings are then given to highlight some existing and potential practical applications for EEIGs. Some of their advantages and disadvantages are briefly mentioned, and a list of questions is provided to assist in determining whether or not an EEIG can support particular businesses' objectives. The chapter is rounded off with a brief summary and conclusions.

EEIGs: A Vehicle for Business

A Truly European Form of Business Enterprise

For the past 20 years, the EC has tried to harmonise company legislation in the Member States in order to bring about a homogeneous commercial environment for industry and investment and in order to invite businesses to cooperate cross-border. A well-known example is the planned European Company Statute ('ECS') which would allow companies to establish an enterprise under uniform European company law.[1] Other initiatives include the Business

[1] In a European Community perspective, the EEIG and ECS were originally thought to go hand in hand, as means to develop and promote cross-border activities and industrial co-operation. The EEIG, a venture which leaves the independence of the different members unaffected, is on a much smaller scale than the ECS. A European company would be established through a cross-border merger of two or more companies in Europe or would work as a holding company for a number of subsidiaries in different Member States, through the creation of a joint subsidiary. It would have its own EC-wide rules for management and operation so that, even more than the EEIG, it would transcend the national frameworks.

Cooperation Network (BC-Net) which assists small and medium-sized enterprises (SMEs) in finding business partners across Europe and the EC Cooperative Research Action for Technology (CRAFT), a programme aimed at technological co-operation between SMEs across frontiers.

In the framework of the single market programme, the EEIG was created to be a truly European form of enterprise in commercial, legal and economic terms. This form of business enterprise has been permitted since 1 July 1989.[2] The EEIG has no precedent and is unique. From a Community perspective, it is considered a first and significant step forward towards reducing major barriers to international co-operation between smaller and larger players in commercial Europe.

For the first time in the EC, businesses can combine forces under a form of enterprise which is recognised uniformly throughout the Community. With a view to a single market without physical, technical and other barriers, the EEIG allows businesses to plan on a pan-European and international, rather than on a national, scale.

In the past, any form of co-operation, such as a joint venture, had to be established according to the laws of one particular Member State. However, due to differences between the Member States' legal systems, conflicts and diverse procedures raised obstacles to pan-European operations. According to the European Commission, the executive arm of the EC, the EEIG is a 'qualitative leap in removing the barriers still standing in the way of cross-frontier co-operation'.[3] Together with the proposed ECS, the EEIG was considered crucial for businesses in Europe to uphold their international competitiveness.

The European Commission's Intentions

The EC legislation establishing the EEIG, is based on a similar form of business enterprise used in France since 1967, called the Groupement d'Intérêt Economique (GIE), or simply Economic Interest Grouping, of which Airbus is the most prominent example. The Commission's most important goal was to provide a flexible and effective tool for cross-border undertakings within the European Community. In order to achieve this, a number of basic principles were established:

1. Simplicity: Creating an EEIG is simple. A minimum of two parties is required and they must have their operations in different EC countries. Having decided to form an EEIG, the Members need only draft a contract and have it

[2] European Community Council Regulation (EEC 1985/2137) (Official Journal, No L 199/1, 31 July 1985).

[3] Bulletin of the European Communities. Supplement 3/87. European Economic Interest Grouping (EEIG), Commission of the European Communities, at p 7.

registered in any Member State. After registration, the EEIG will be regarded uniformly throughout the EC.

2. Accessibility: The Commission's goal was to create a form of business enterprise which is as open and as accessible as possible. Companies incorporated under different national rules or with a different legal status, government bodies, universities, or individuals could all be Members of the *same* EEIG. Any combination of the various national types of private business corporations (such as NV, SA, AG, BVBA, GmbH, etc) found throughout the Member States may form an EEIG; and equally any of these may enter into an EEIG with a government research laboratory or a private individual, such as an independent consultant.

However, on a national basis, the Member States may limit or prohibit membership of an EEIG for certain activities which fall under the auspices of a professional body or other regulatory authority governing the activities of a particular sector. For instance, in Germany, notaries are not allowed to be a member of an EEIG. The same holds for bailiffs in Belgium. Also in that Member State, public credit institutions may only participate in an EEIG after they have received authorisation to do so from the national supervising authority.

With respect to accessibility, it is interesting to note that, following the establishment of the EEIG, Spain proposed and Belgium introduced national Economic Interest Groupings (EIG). A national EIG may be instrumental in promoting cross-border activities, since the members accustomed to this form of enterprise may ultimately seek international links.

3. Flexibility: The Commission wanted to ensure a high degree of flexibility for participation. Not only European companies, but also EC-based subsidiaries of US or Japanese companies may be members of an EEIG. For individuals, membership is open irrespective of nationality provided that the person's economic activities are carried out within the European Community. Examples are agricultural, craft, industrial or commercial activities, as well as professional or management services.

4. Mobility: From the moment an EEIG is registered in one Member State, it is considered established throughout the EC. In practice, this means that an EEIG may carry out its activities over the entire territory of the EC, including in those countries which have not yet set up the practical mechanism for registration. Moreover, an EEIG may easily change its registered address.

5. Activities: The objectives and activities of the EEIG must be related and ancillary to the economic activities of each of the Members. However, 'ancillary' and 'related' are broad terms which may be widely interpreted. Nevertheless, the EEIG may not replace but only extend or supplement existing activities of its Members. Within this framework, the EEIG may be used for anything.

In creating this tool for cross-border collaboration, the Commission had a number of target groups and uses in mind. The so-called liberal professions, such as lawyers or architects, were certainly amongst them. Another target group was the vast number of small and medium-sized enterprises (SMEs) which exist across Europe. An important activity which the Commission had in mind was research and development ('R&D'). The EEIG also offers an ideal opportunity for large corporations to pool resources. This is important in view of EC anti-trust rules since EEIGs may permit rival corporate giants to co-operate in specific areas without being accused of distorting competition or preventing free trade within the Community.

Suitability of EEIGs for Cross-Frontier Co-operation

In the run-up to the completion of the internal market and beyond, the EEIG is well suited to promote pan-European ventures. Until now, transnational commercial activity has often been prohibitively cumbersome or risky especially for SMEs. Partnerships have in the past served as the major co-operative vehicle between SMEs or individuals. However, these did not provide any real guarantees for third parties or for their participants. A formal partnership, such as a contractual joint venture for project or equipment financing, was usually a complex and difficult affair to operate. A more rigid vehicle, such as a merger, could be too far-reaching. When larger corporations combined resources, they could not do so without having to worry unduly about possible anti-trust allegations.

The EEIG, in contrast, permits its Members considerable freedom. Under this form of enterprise, businesses can combine part of their economic activities while preserving their financial independence and autonomy. In doing so, the EEIG provides a structured framework which may be kept very light. In this respect, an EEIG could also serve as a half-way house between an informal partnership and a formal joint venture or merger and pave the way from co-operation to eventual integration of its Members.

The EEIG is not only useful to SMEs but also for large companies, and for smaller and larger companies working together. Some smaller companies produce highly specialised products (eg in interactive communication techniques). It may be of added value for a larger company to work with a smaller one in order to do collaborative research within a specified project. The smaller company, in turn, acquires access to a large network for use, marketing and sale of its products.

Clearly, this form of enterprise is an important asset for SMEs because it allows activities to be undertaken which would otherwise have been too expensive, too large or too risky for an individual company. Examples of such activities are the joint purchase of an aircraft, a building or manufacturing plant. As will be shown in the case study below, the same is true for large corporations which, for instance, wish to promote the results of certain R&D projects and share the costs and risks.

The European Commission found the EEIG to be 'a genuine management tool'[4] which offers the potential to avoid duplicative efforts and save expenses. In general it is hoped that this will facilitate the seizure of opportunities to uphold and improve the competitive position of European businesses.

Suitable Business Activities for an EEIG

What does Using an EEIG Mean in Practice?

The most important characteristics of an EEIG are that it is pan-European and that it has a very flexible supporting structure. Of great importance is how the contract, forming the EEIG, is drafted. Its objectives and activities define the general commitment of the members. To this end, the EEIG may buy property, find funds, employ people, etc. A separate meeting of the Members is not necessary for each decision as may be the case with an informal project partnership.

Using an EEIG makes it easier to operate internationally. It is left to the Members' imagination to facilitate and develop economic activities and to improve or increase their results. Members of existing EEIGs say that operating as a single entity, both within and outside the EC, adds stature to their business. For smaller companies, it holds the potential for commercial networks comparable to those of multinational corporations.

An EEIG may have several activities and most of the existing ones do have many objectives (eg education, exchange of information, marketing, etc). Contrary to what is sometimes mistakenly assumed, an EEIG may operate outside the European Community. For example, an EEIG may have the promotion of its products for export to Japan as its main activity. In this way, the EEIG may be a suitable vehicle to approach large, new or distant markets.

This form of enterprise aids the provision of higher levels of customer service. For instance rebates, faster supply and more integrated after-sales service across the EC may be possible.

How have Companies Used EEIGs?

Initial acceptance of the EEIG by commercial Europe has been somewhat hesitant. This may be due to a lack of awareness, especially among individuals and one-person companies, of the existence of the EEIG. But an equally likely explanation of its relatively restricted early use may lie in a certain reticence on

[4] Séverine Israël, 'The EEIG - A major step forward for Community Law', Company Lawyer, Vol 9, No 1 (1988), p 22.

the part of the business community towards the unknown and specifically to a legal entity which is not an established part of national legal systems.

Early EEIGs were concentrated in the service sector, particularly in the fields of legal advice and public relations. Undoubtedly, for these professions, establishing an EEIG was also a means to acquire valuable experience in this form of enterprise which could be passed on to clients. In addition, a number of relatively small enterprises found the EEIG suited to their needs. Gradually, the number of EEIGs has increased and its applications have been extended. Examples of some of the first applications for EEIGs were in joint purchase and sale of goods, freight forwarding and consulting. Medium-sized and larger corporations have now also begun to exploit its potential.

Regardless of the type of activity under consideration, the threat of increased competition is the predominant motive driving businesses to establish an EEIG. This is true for large corporations (see case study on Vision 1250 EEIG) as well as among SMEs. Both consider the EEIG as a means to provide extensive and more integrated services to customers.

Using the EEIG, companies and individuals feel able to strengthen their competitive position and increase their existing market shares. EEIG Members find that their participation in ventures of this kind provides a stimulating and dynamic means of building and projecting a European image. In their attack on new markets, Members report that this form of enterprise is taken seriously by their business partners throughout the world.

Table 1 on the following page lists the early types of EEIGs (May 1990). The activities of these EEIGs illustrate the usefulness of this vehicle for a great number of ventures. A large number of the existing EEIGs fall within the broad discipline of the service sector. This was not entirely what the drafters of the EC legislation had in mind. However, according to the Commission's services,

Table 1: Nature of EEIGs

ACTIVITY	APPROXIMATE NUMBER
Agricultural Commodities Trading	39
Consulting	8
Marketing	7
Law Firms	6
Joint R&D	3
Environment (Water Quality)	3
Audiovisual	2
Import/Export	2
Finance	2
Real Estate	1
Training	1
Transport	1
Export	1
Paint Manufacturing	1

SOURCE: *Price Waterhouse Consultants*

new EEIGs are being established, for instance in the field of R&D, which is more in line with the original intentions of the Commission. In keeping with recent trends in the industry, three EEIGs focus on environmental issues. As companies and individuals continue to discover the EEIG and its potential, further diversification in its practical uses should emerge.

Table 2 (on p 16) provides an overview of the most important existing EEIGs with an indication of their membership, if available, and country of registration.

It shows that EEIGs are registered in many EC Member States.[5] Managers of some of the existing EEIGs report that they preferred a location because of its physical convenience. Obviously, for export or transport EEIGs, Antwerp or Rotterdam are well positioned. Sometimes, the place for registration was chosen because it was the home country of the largest Member. So far, the majority of EEIGs have been registered in Belgium, the Netherlands, France, the UK and Germany. But Denmark and Spain have also registered EEIGs. For a more detailed discussion of the selection of the country(ies) of registration, see Chapter 3.

Case Study: *Vision* 1250 *EEIG*

On 11 July 1990, an EEIG called Vision 1250 was officially presented at a special event organised by the European Commission and Parliament and the Council of Europe in Strasbourg, France. This EEIG has as its Members a cross-section of the television programme production industry and includes consumer electronics and studio equipment manufacturers, public commercial broadcasters, independent producers, film production operations and possibly transmission companies. Its objectives are to produce High Definition Television (HDTV) programmes, to down-convert and transmit them and to demonstrate the European HDTV standard.

The creation of Vision 1250 EEIG was the final result of an ambitious concept initiated in 1988. The EC Heads of State and Government, at European summits in Rhodes (1988) and Strasbourg (1989) emphasised the global importance of HDTV for strengthening Europe's cultural heritage but also its significance for the EC's electronics as well as audiovisual and broadcasting industries. This was reflected in a decision adopted by the EC Council of Ministers setting forth a comprehensive strategy for introducing HDTV services in the Community.

This strategy was aimed at:

1. Developing the necessary technology and equipment to launch HDTV services.

[5] For those countries where formal legislation on registering is not yet in place, registration can be achieved through, for instance, national administrative circulars addressed to the commercial registers to accept registration of EEIGs.

Table 2: Existing EEIGs

EEIG	MEMBERS	REGISTERED IN
Name	Number	EC Country
ARCHITECTURO	2	B
Associated Consultants Europe	5	NL
Association des Producteurs Européens de Bananes	3	B
Association of Commercial Television	5	B
B.E.P.I.A.S. (on issues re Soviet Automobiles)	10	B
Coopération Européenne de Marketing	4	B
de Morgan Profi	2	UK
DIFF EUROPE	2	B
EEIGs on meat trading in general (39)	2	NL
Euro Activ Comb & Co.	n/a	D
Euro Asconet	6	NL
Euro Büro	2	D
Euro Marine	n/a	F
EUROADVICE	5	B
EUROGRAPH	3	B
Eurohypo	2	B
Eurojurist	7	F
Euromarine 7	4	B
Europe Business Development	5	NL
European Advertising Lawyers Association	9	D
European Combined Overseas Forwarders	5	B
European Law Firm	3	NL
European Management Group	2	NL
European Procurement Agents	7	UK
First European Taxation Group	2	NL
Galathée	n/a	F
GELABOR	3	F
Group 92	n/a	F
Independent Paint Companies Europe	4	E
JÜROP	9	D
Miljøteknik	2	DK
Pannone De Backer	5	B
Parlex Group of European Lawyers	6	UK
Pole de Développement Ibérique	2	B
RESULT	2	NL
SODIFOR	n/a	F
Vision 1250	14+	B

n/a = not available

Source: *Price Waterhouse Consultants*

2. Promoting the worldwide adoption of the European standard for originating and transmitting HDTV programmes.
3. Introducing HDTV services in the Community in a timely fashion.
4. Achieving the capability and necessary experience to produce HDTV films and television programmes which are competitive in the global market place.

The setting up of Vision 1250 EEIG, registered in Brussels, was backed and co-ordinated by the Commission. At the 11 July press conference, the role of this EEIG was outlined by the Commissioners of Research and Audiovisual Affairs. It is a pro-active measure which from the manufacturers' viewpoint is aimed at developing a European standard HDTV market and which, for the users, should provide access to limited resources in a pre-market situation.

The main investment is the cost of the HDTV equipment which is given on loan to and for use by the Members in order to attain the EEIG's principal goal. The equipment is paid by a committee of sponsors which includes the Commission, and the Dutch, French and German governments (budget allocation for the period 1990–92 is approximately ECU 120 million, including 12.7 million for 1991 drawn from the EC budget). The French Economic Interest Grouping, International HD, will be phased out through incorporation of its assets in Vision 1250 EEIG. Similar pooling of resources was seen as essential to stave off competition from the Japanese HDTV industry. It was felt that giving equipment on loan, based on a schedule set up by the EEIG's director general, would overcome a situation in which EC manufacturers could not provide equipment systems for HDTV programme production for free to users, like the Japanese competitors did.

The objective is worldwide adoption of the European Standard for HDTV production and transmission as soon as possible. According to the formation contract, the EEIG's activities are meant to ensure the smooth and rapid transition from prototype use to actual HDTV services operating to European standards.

The Grouping's task is focused on establishing and managing fixed and mobile HDTV facilities which will be made available to broadcasters, television and film production companies and software producers within the EC. These facilities will have a full range of HDTV production equipment (demonstration is secondary use) operating to the European HDTV production standards and will include all the components of an HDTV system from studio equipment to transmission. Programme production will be undertaken for commercial distribution either in down-converted form (PAL or SECAM) or in their original format. For example, Vision 1250 covered the 1990 Football (soccer) World Championships. Other pilot projects include coverage of the Olympic Games in Albertville and Barcelona together with the 1992 World Exhibition in Seville. Users' observations on the equipment were fed back to the equipment manufacturers to ensure a rapid ergonomic evolution of the equipment. Having producers and users in one Grouping obviously is a major advantage. Besides the HDTV production and demonstration, the EEIG also provides for training, technical advice and equipment maintenance.

The list of actual and potential collaborators is impressive and includes four to six equipment manufacturers, about 20 public broadcasters (European Broadcasting Union members) and independent producers made out of commercial broadcasters, production houses and film makers. Members pay a flat-rate subscription fee. Philips, Thomson and Bosch, the driving forces behind developing the European HDTV Standard are all Members of Vision 1250 EEIG. Other founding Members include BC, British Satellite Broadcasting, Thames Television and Laser Creation (UK), BHD TV, Nokia, Unitel and BTS (Germany), France Télécom, SFT and OFRT (France) and RAI (Italy).

Why this particular case study?

Vision 1250 EEIG was singled out because of its task to influence and determine the further evolution of European HDTV and for its potential impact on the audiovisual, broadcasting and electronics sectors in the EC. Moreover, its success in promoting the European HDTV system is likely to be of major significance on a global economic scale. Significantly, the EEIG form of business enterprise permits the largest European producers of television and related equipment to work together on a special purpose project without raising fears of monopoly or cartel action since the entire operation would be transparent. This particular EEIG also confirms that this form of enterprise is a very potent tool for business in promoting a product or any innovative technologies to new markets in Europe and the rest of the world.

Typical Areas of Application

This section gives a further picture of possible applications for EEIGs in a commercial environment. Commercial uses are illustrated with examples of existing EEIGs and these are set in the wider context of how this vehicle can support and promote the strategic corporate objectives of its Members. The EEIGs described below illustrate the broad range of activities which may be undertaken via the medium of an EEIG.

The Regulation establishing the EEIG mentions no specific commercial uses for the Grouping. However, Commission officials had a number of applications in mind when drafting the legislation. Suitable professional or commercial activities were thought to include joint promotion and development of services, such as legal or financial advice, or management consultancy, joint tendering for large contracts, especially for public procurement, and forming combinations for other types of procurement bidding or marketing, and for R&D.

Services

The first EEIG to be created was the European Law Firm (ELF) established on 3 July 1989 between a Dutch law firm, a German lawyer and a Belgian lawyer. It was set up not to practice law itself, but to support, facilitate and develop the legal and economic activities of its Members and specifically to promote co-operation in the scientific, trade and financial fields. Its objectives expressly include co-operation with law firms and other organisations outside the EC.

Another lawyers' EEIG, the Parlex Group of European Lawyers, has the objective of increasing the quality, reliability and efficiency of cross-border legal advice. Through this vehicle, the British, Danish, Irish, Dutch, Portuguese and German Members hope to improve co-operation among lawyers from different European countries. By and large the same motivations drove the five members of another consortium of legal firms, Pannone De Backer EEIG, in pooling their expertise in a bid to give a competitive boost to their business. Quite a number of European lawyers have joined forces in order to compete with US lawyers, who have established offices in European cities to practice EC law.

These legal services Groupings constitute a classic application for the EEIG. By reason of their professional or national bar rules, most liberal professions, such as lawyers, were limited in their freedom to arrange a structured framework for cross-border operations. At an EEIG conference, held in April 1989, a representative of an EEIG combining eight law firms, mentioned that before the advent of the EEIG, law firms had to enter into bilateral agreements in order to co-operate with one another. Due to the number of firms involved, this would have produced a burdensome total of 72 bilateral contracts which would have been an exacting arrangement even given the strong commitment to a multinational partnership. Thanks to the EEIG, only one contract is necessary between all eight Members.

Obviously, EEIGs are not only for lawyers. The expanding service sector presents numerous opportunities for using an EEIG. Examples include the First European Taxation Group EEIG, a tax management consultancy and Coopération Européenne de Marketing EEIG, a team of consultants which pinpoints potential markets for the Members' products.

The Association of Commercial Television in Europe EEIG, a Grouping of five television stations in the EC, serves as a platform for airing and developing ideas with commercial potential for the audiovisual industry in the Community.

The Architecturo EEIG focuses on publicity campaigns and public relations exercises throughout Europe.

The real estate and property finance consultancy, de Morgan Profi EEIG, provides its clients with a comprehensive advisory service on portfolio management, investment opportunities, property valuation and associated activities. In offering this integrated package, the emphasis is on joint promotion and marketing.

An additional application, suitable for the EEIG, is the whole range of promotional and management support activities for small and medium-sized enterprises, particularly in view of the single market challenge. This is exactly what the five partners of Europe Business Development EEIG had in mind when they set out to jointly provide a wide range of administrative support facilities, which for SMEs represent considerable overheads.

The EEIG is also ideal for representation activities, including the preparation of joint requests for EC subsidies or loans. Part of the activity of RESULT EEIG is directed at obtaining loans. Other possibilities are cross-border lobbying, eg for organisations importing Soviet automobiles (BEPIAS EEIG), market research, international sales promotion, image building, and publicity.

Joint bidding

European Commission officials frequently cite joint tendering for large contracts, in particular for public procurement, as a reason for creating an EEIG. The EEIG offers better opportunities to suppliers. In the past, they usually needed to use a joint venture, or were subcontractors. In the case of an EEIG, all suppliers are Members of the EEIG unit which can have a single contract with the client.

For its seven members, European Procurement Agents EEIG acts as a forum for discussion between them and with the Commission, in particular with respect to providing services to the African, Caribbean and Pacific States under contracts financed by the European Community, such as the European Development Fund.

Research and development

Large and small companies can both take advantage of R&D EEIGs. They permit combined research in high technology fields such as electronics and biotechnology, or eminently complicated areas such as the environment, a field in which EUROMARINE 7 EEIG is active. However, these R&D projects can also be on a small scale. This is the case for Eurograph EEIG which promotes research in written and audiovisual communications to assist in the modernising and restructuring of the printing industry in Europe. The Groupement Européen de Laboratoires or GELABOR EEIG was established to pool resources for fundamental research in veterinary products and to improve its position in this market segment.

Transport

A good example of an EEIG in the area of transport is the European Combined Overseas Forwarders EEIG. As the name suggests, its five members are freight forwarders for road, sea and air transport companies. Apart from promoting and developing the activities and co-operation of the members, this EEIG's tasks include providing administrative, commercial, legal and fiscal advice to international clients. The EEIG's goal is to take care of all the activities which are routinely connected with the purchase and sale of goods for import and export, including brokerage, freight handling, shipping and insurance. The wide range of support functions, vital for this business, tends to consume considerable resources. Using the EEIG vehicle saves money because it is a one-stop shop for services. Transport EEIGs are likely to become more common as a result of the eventual elimination of customs formalities within the EC. EEIGs for distribution and warehousing are a likely response to the advent of an integrated logistics industry on a European scale.

Export

Combining resources is crucial in the highly competitive and demanding export sector. The planned Export Focus (crafts) EEIG illustrates this. Its main objective is to increase the export of a wide range of specialty products from various regions of Europe into the world market. The means by which the Members intend to open the Japanese market, their main target, include export missions, public relations, a planned European trading house for their Members and an office in Japan.

In December 1989, a large number of EEIGs, registered in Rotterdam, were established for trading in importing and exporting meat and clearing it through customs. The Dutch, Belgian, French and German members of this EEIG are competitors. In anticipation of the completion of the single market, they set up these EEIGs in a bid to establish a co-operative network between them rather than competing each other out of business in a completed internal market.

In this way, an EEIG can be used for trading, export, import and related activities in many sectors of industry.

Training

An EEIG use which has considerable potential is the establishment of training courses. This is the case with European Management Programme EEIG, which specialises in the provision of continuing education of Euro-managers, a service which is complementary to its Members' existing business training programmes.

Joint manufacturing

Thanks to the planned elimination of technical, physical and fiscal barriers, increased need for joint processing and manufacturing is likely. In this respect, the EEIG may be very suitable for setting up experimental production and pilot programmes and schemes for new or speciality products that are developed jointly. Based on the words and context of the EEIG Regulation, it should be possible as well to engage in permanent production of certain goods as long as that particular manufacturing is ancillary to the Members' activities. Amongst the objectives of the Independent Paint Companies Europe EEIG is the common manufacturing of paint products resulting from jointly developed technology. This particular EEIG may be influential because in the recent past the German cartel authorities appear to have objected to a consortium of photographers which wanted to set up an EEIG for a common procurement shop which was close to permanent performance.

Information

As the European chess board becomes even more complex, a crucial area will be the flow of data and knowledge. An EEIG to promote the distribution of information on the European Community in France is planned. Importantly, this EEIG is promoted by the EC and most notably by the Presidents of both the European Commission and the Parliament. There is a market here for management consultancies and similar businesses.

The EEIG for local governments

Untapped so far is the use that can potentially be made of the EEIG form of enterprise by regional, provincial, county, local or similar governments to assist businesses in their constituencies to seize the opportunities of the single market or to help them overcome possible threats.

Advantages and Disadvantages of the EEIG

Advantages

European dimension

In contrast to the other possible forms of transnational venture, the EEIG is a modern form of joint venture in which an organisation is not so restricted by national frameworks. The most significant advantage of this form of enterprise is its European scope. It allows companies and individuals to form a flexible relationship on a pan-European level and to create a European image.

Economies of scale

Involving less risk than for an individual player, investments are possible on a larger scale. Exploitation of existing markets may be easier and return on investment better assured. EEIGs may take advantage of combined overheads and coupling of efforts thereby reducing costs, building leaner structures and increasing efficiency.

Any national EIG can be a member of an EEIG providing a tremendous potential for combined sourcing, resources and pooling of activities which may markedly increase the venture's competitive edge in the market.

Built-in capacity for quick decision-making and for grabbing market opportunities

Contrary to other joint venture type arrangements which, for instance require that national managerial rules be followed, the EEIG may be managed and run in a very flexible way.

Rather than having to adopt a possibly burdensome management structure, the EEIG Members can freely decide how much power they grant the manager(s) who will run the venture. Choosing an individual management mode, specified in the contract, provides room for a different style of management, relying on trust and co-operative behaviour. For instance, Members may have a framework agreement on how to distribute the work in case a joint project comes through. According to Members of existing EEIGs, similar flexibility allows for the EEIG manager to take decisions very rapidly (eg responding to an invitation to tender). In this way, so Members say, the physical distance between them, which may create problems for co-ordination, does not become an issue.

Existing Members also feel that the EEIG's flexible management allows for a better response to competitive pressures. More so than other forms of joint venture agreements, such as an association of companies for a particular project (usually dissociated after the work is finished), its management structure supports an ongoing market-led approach. It must not be forgotten that the EEIG is a form of enterprise which, as mentioned, is recognised uniformly all over the Community. The absence of any such vehicle was singled out by EEIG Members as a barrier to doing business across borders. For SMEs in particular, it was exacting to explore markets, other than their home base. For larger corporations, it is an added dimension in adapting their businesses continuously to changing operational realities.

New markets

The penetration of new EC or foreign markets is made less of an adventure by a joint approach, such as an EEIG. By virtue of its multi-national membership, the EEIG promotes better appreciation of national differences, likely to persist within the single market, and may facilitate the entry, or better access, into an additional EC country market.

Synergies

Through its close links among its Members, the EEIG allows considerable synergies in terms of market knowledge, and ways and means for sourcing and supply. This is vital especially for SMEs because of their size and limited resources. However, large corporations also benefit, as is clear from Vision 1250.

A single business partner

When negotiating with an EEIG, the customer has the advantage of only having to sign one contract to acquire a full range of services. This one-stop shop concept is likely to become increasingly attractive to business.

Disadvantages

There are certain drawbacks to using an EEIG. However, not all the features under this heading are necessarily negative and certain restrictions enhance the credibility of the EEIG.

Competition restraint

Clearly, an EEIG may not be created to avoid EC competition legislation. If in doubt, members of a planned EEIG should discuss this with the European Commission who, on a case-by-case basis, may award an exemption, eg for research and development.

Not for profit only

An EEIG may be instrumental in increasing the competitiveness and business results of the Members but may not be created solely for the purpose of making profits for itself. If this were the aim of the venture, then the EEIG would probably not be the right vehicle.

Maximum 500 employees

The EEIG may not employ more than 500 persons. If the activities of the venture are very labour intensive, this form of enterprise may not be suitable. However, the limit of 500 employees is not necessarily an adverse factor. With modern automation techniques 500 people can achieve a great deal.

Registration formalities

Each of the EC Member States needs to set up a national machinery for registration of EEIGs. The procedures differ from country to country and some States have been slow to establish a machinery for registration. From a practical point of view, it may be worth contacting the relevant national authorities to find out whether an EEIG can be registered and how. Some of their addresses are given in the Table of Member States' Registration Formalities in Appendix II of this book.

National legislation

As mentioned above, the EEIG is recognised uniformly throughout the Community. Nevertheless, the Members must be aware of national laws and in particular those of the country where the EEIG is registered. A given Member State may require, for example, that the EEIG complies with its accounting rules, and national differences in employment, social security and fiscal laws should also be considered.

Existing EEIGs resolve these issues by relying on the Member's knowledge of their national laws. It is not hard to see how this 'disadvantage' may be turned into a benefit because it allows the Members to choose the 'best' set of national rules for the EEIG.

Taxation rules

Taxation of the EEIG is transparent in that any profits or losses of the Grouping are allocated to the Members. However, it must be borne in mind that some elements related to corporate or personal income taxation may be rather complex. Chapter 4 provides further insight into these aspects.

Joint and several liability of Members

The EEIG form of enterprise is not a free ride for its Members vis-à-vis their business partners. The joint and several liability of Members complements the absence of a minimum capital for the EEIG. However, none of the Members of existing EEIGs perceive this obligation to be a severe burden but consider it as part of their commitment to the venture. Moreover, it enhances the credibility of the EEIG in the eyes of third parties.

Check-List

Before considering establishing an EEIG with one or more partners, or becoming a member of an existing EEIG, a number of key elements need to be determined. They are reviewed below in two separate sets of questions which are ranked in order of importance. Combined, they represent important commercial reasons for using an EEIG as opposed to any other kind of joint venture arrangement.

The first questions are directed to a *single* company, institution or individual (referred to as an 'organisation') and should be reviewed first. If your organisation is positive about all the questions, one or more like-minded partners must be found (Chapter 5 provides guidance on this). Assuming that these have been found, a different set of points needs to be addressed before going into practicalities. These questions pertain to the EEIG activities and should ideally be reviewed by the prospective EEIG Members *together*.

If all the answers are affirmative, consider using an EEIG. However, the checklist is only a guide to determining whether the EEIG is a suitable commercial option for a particular organisation or activity. To obtain a more detailed overview, consult an expert in this field. The same holds when some answers are negative because with proper changes, this form of enterprise may still be possible.

Questions to be Answered by a Single Organisation

1. An EEIG invites international activities, ie beyond the boundaries of a given national territory, between organisations of different national origin. Is your organisation interested in operating cross-frontier within the European Community and/or outside the EC, together with other organisations (partners)?
2. The EEIG is simple to set up (contract and registration) and has a built-in capacity for flexible management and structures. Is your organisation interested in such a non-cumbersome tool to operate across borders?
3. The EEIG is uniformly recognised all over the EC, provides the freedom to avoid burdensome structures and has a large potential for swift business interaction with market forces. Does your organisation prefer its business decisions to be driven by similar forces rather than by individual countries' regulatory frameworks?
4. An EEIG provides an added dimension to an organisation's thinking and operation. It invites prospective Members to look not only at the domestic market but also beyond, in Europe and/or globally. Is your organisation interested in promoting and developing such thinking and operational behaviour?

Questions to be Reviewed by the Prospective EEIG Members

1. Are the intended partners established in the EC or do they carry out commerical activities within the EC?
2. Do the national governing bodies or regulatory authorities of certain professions, institutions or sectors of industry allow membership of an EEIG?
3. Are the intended EEIG activities ancillary or supplementary and thus related to the activities of *all* the intended Members?
4. Will the number of employees in the EEIG stay below 500?

Summary and Conclusions

This chapter is based on existing EEIGs and how this EC vehicle has been transposed into business life. As a new optional form of cross-frontier enterprise, the EEIG has had considerable success, mostly thanks to its overall flexibility. A preliminary assessment of the practical applications of the EEIG as a novel form of enterprise strongly suggests that it is a truly useful tool for any joint venture, co-operation, partnership, pooling and/or cost saving arrangements.

As noted in the last part of this chapter, some disadvantages were identified. Undoubtedly, it will always remain hard for any form of enterprise, designed to facilitate cross-frontier ventures, to accommodate the very different needs and concerns of businesses operating in the Community. However, these minor flaws do not appear to deter corporations or individuals from using an EEIG. The examples above indicated that the common sense and imagination of business in Europe are overriding. Also, as was shown in the case study, the European Commission actively supports and promotes the EEIG and Commission officials are commited to the success of this form of business enterprise.

Having explored possible commercial uses of the EEIG vehicle, the next chapter explains the legal elements that will need to be considered when establishing this corporate form.

CHAPTER THREE
LEGAL AND PRACTICAL CONSIDERATIONS

Introduction

This chapter seeks to give an overview of material matters that ideally should be considered when forming an EEIG. It does not attempt to be a full analysis or comparison of the legal means of economic co-operation or integration between businesses in Europe whether through a contractual joint venture, a partnership, a company or an EEIG.

The great strengths of an EEIG are the flexibility of its structure and means of operation and the fact that it is a legal entity in its own right. This latter feature of course is not the case with a contractual joint venture or a partnership being used as a joint venture vehicle. As a result, an EEIG is able directly:

(1) to enter into contracts on its own behalf;
(2) to own property in its own name;
(3) to sue and be sued in its own name; and
(4) ultimately, if the venture is not a success, to be wound up.

An EEIG may be a very suitable means of co-operation and cost sharing between businesses in different countries where funding for the venture can be provided by the Members and where the business risks associated with the venture are low. Since an EEIG may only be used for a purpose ancillary to the business and activities of its Members, it is not a suitable vehicle for setting up some completely new venture which has no direct connection with its Members. In such circumstances it would probably be more appropriate to use a company. The EEIG is the same as a partnership in two ways: first, it has the advantage of not requiring any initial capital to be subscribed to it, and secondly it has the disadvantage of its Members having joint and several liability for its debts.

The EEIG incorporates certain features of other traditional methods of forming joint ventures. It is similar to a contractual joint venture in the sense that the parties are free to agree a wide variety of terms, but it also has many of the characteristics and disciplines of a partnership or company.

References in this chapter to the 'Regulation' are to the European Community Council Regulation (EEC 1985/2137) and references to the 'Statutory

Instrument' are to the United Kingdom European Economic Interest Grouping Regulations (1989/638). The Regulation came into force in the European Community on 25 July 1985 and provided that each of the EC countries may set up the necessary machinery for the registration of Groupings in their territories and the disclosure of certain matters relating to Groupings, and may apply or adopt any laws, regulations or administrative measures which do not conflict with the scope or objectives of the Regulation. To this end, on 1 July 1989, the Statutory Instrument was brought into force in Great Britain (that is to say in England, Wales and Scotland) and governs the formation and operation of EEIGs in such territory. (A statutory instrument in similar terms having application to Northern Ireland was brought into force on 17 July 1990.) In the event of a conflict between the Regulation and a national law, the provisions of the Regulation prevail.

Not all Member States of the EC have implemented national legislation enabling the registration of an EEIG in that State. At the time of writing (mid-August 1990) the following countries had enacted and enforced appropriate national legislation: Eire, Belgium, Denmark, France, Germany, Great Britain, The Netherlands, Northern Ireland and Portugal. Legislation in Spain is in draft form, and is expected shortly to be enacted. Draft legislation has been prepared in Italy but as yet no draft legislation has been published in Greece or Luxembourg. Appendix II gives brief details of the legistation relating to EEIGs in each of the EC states. Since the legal systems in Scotland and Northern Ireland differ from that in England and Wales, separate legal advice should be taken in such jurisdiction before seeking to register an EEIG having its official address there. It is somewhat anomalous that the Statutory Instrument relates to England, Wales and Scotland; evidently the system of EEIG registration in each of the two jurisdictions is to be the same. It is unclear what the effect would be of purporting to register an EEIG in a Member State which has no machinery in place. The safest option is to register an EEIG in a country, such as England and Wales, which has adopted the Regulation into its national law.

This chapter deals principally with an EEIG registered in England and Wales. However, because the EEIG is governed primarily by an EC Regulation, the position of an EEIG registered in another EC country will in many ways be comparable to the one described below.

The Role of the EEIG Formation Agreement

The cornerstone of the EEIG is the Formation Agreement between its Members. The Regulation provides a skeleton of basic terms that must be included in the Formation Agreement. It is for the parties to flesh out those basic terms as they think fit, provided they do not contravene the Regulation, the Statutory Instrument or relevant local or EC law. The check-list of clauses in an EEIG agreement in Appendix I sets out those provisions the Regulation requires to be included in the Formation Agreement and those that it may be desirable to include.

The EEIG, being an entirely new entity, does not as yet enjoy a sound body of jurisprudence relating to its regulation and operation upon which its prospective Members can rely if they have failed to address a particular matter in the Formation Agreement either by oversight or by choice. By contrast, if a company or a partnership in any EC country had been the chosen business vehicle, there would be many precedents and comprehensive legislation which would govern in the event of the document of incorporation or partnership agreement being silent on a particular point. It may be that, with time, the Regulation will be considered by the European Court of Justice, and the meaning of certain of its provisions will be clarified or indeed construed in particular ways, which would lead to greater certainty for those embarking upon setting up an EEIG. At the same time, however, separate bodies of jurisprudence may develop in each Member State, leading the treatment of an EEIG to vary according to the country in which it is registered. It follows that, if the parties fail to reach agreement on any matter relating to the constitution and/or operation of the Grouping, there is currently a legal lacuna. Accordingly there is a very strong argument in favour of the EEIG Formation Agreement being a relatively detailed document which precisely sets out the intentions of the parties, in order to create practical and legal certainty. Indeed, within the limits of the Regulation the parties may write their own 'law' to govern their business affairs.

The disadvantages of drawing up a lengthy Formation Agreement however, are as follows. First, that the Formation Agreement must be registered at the Companies Registry, and is therefore available for public inspection. The European Economic Interest Grouping (Fees) Amendment Regulations 1990/1203 came into force in the UK on 7 June 1990, and increased the fee for inspection of documents at the Registry to £2.75. Delivery by post of extracts of the Register was increased to £5.00 for each extract. This would always be the case if the parties chose to use a company as their vehicle for operation. However, an EEIG, unlike a company, is under no obligation to file annual accounts at the Companies Registry and therefore offers a more private method of collaboration. Secondly, the circumstances, time and budget available for formation may dictate a simpler document.

Thirdly, while many people do not relish the prospect of negotiating and drafting relatively long contracts, in most civil law jurisdictions this is probably less necessary than in common law jurisdictions, such as England, Wales and Eire, where longer business contracts are rather more usual. The reason for this is that civil law contracts have a greater tendency than common law contracts to make statutory references, rather than repeating certain provisions verbatim.

Finally, while lawyers may advise their clients to strive for certainty in their business dealings, some businessmen may not wish to be constrained at the outset by detailed agreement and may prefer to allow the business relations to evolve and develop in a flexible manner over time. Each of the views of certainty and flexibility have their merit. The more important the venture is to the various parties, the greater sense there is in striving for certainty by negotiating a more detailed agreement. That does not mean however that a venture of relatively small importance to the parties should not be adequately considered at the outset.

Major Matters to Consider in Forming an EEIG

In forming an EEIG, the following main points should be borne in mind:

(1) Where should the EEIG be formed and registered?
(2) Who may set up an EEIG?
(3) Who are to be the fellow Members of the EEIG?
(4) How shall the Grouping be funded?
(5) What provisions should the Formation Agreement contain?
(6) What competition law provisions affect EEIGs?
(7) What are the registration procedures for a Grouping in each of the EC Member States?

Each of these points and many subsidiary and detailed points on formation of the Grouping are set out below. The Formation Agreement should set out the Members' agreed answers to these questions and include the necessary mechanics to realise the Members' wishes. The registration formalities for each Member State are summarised, insofar as they are known at the time of writing, in Appendix II.

(1) Where should the EEIG be Formed and Registered?

Is the Regulation in Force in the Proposed Country of Registration?

The first thing to establish is whether ancillary national legislation in relation to the Regulation has been adopted in the proposed country of registration. If so, does such national law (whether pre-dating the Regulation or implementing it) permit the proposed Members to participate in a Grouping? For example, Belgian law has provided that Belgian bailiffs and public financial institutions may not participate in an EEIG, wherever it may be registered.

Which Country's National Law should Govern the Grouping?

The Regulation seems to provide that the governing law for all questions other than those relating to status or capacity of persons will be the private international law of the country in which the Grouping has its official address.

The status or nationality of the persons entering into the Formation Agreement may require certain provisions to be included. For example, for the contract to be legally enforceable in Italy the Italian Civil Code provides that certain clauses in a contract governed by Italian law must be *specifically agreed to* by the parties (for example, a clause depriving the Italian courts of jurisdiction by agreeing to arbitration in London). Failure to obtain such specific agreement renders such clauses unenforceable. It follows that if there is any likelihood of the Formation Agreement being governed by Italian law in the future, expert Italian legal advice should be sought as to which clauses require specific agreement, and such agreement should be sought by all the parties. Clearly, other jurisdictions may have similar laws worthy of consideration in this way. Further, it was apparently the draughtsmen's intention that the law governing the Formation Agreement would be the domestic law of that country. This may be in order to protect the creditors of the Grouping whose claims may be defeated if a Grouping ceases to be registered in one country and is registered in a new country. However, the relevant provisions are open to various interpretations. It is hoped that this ambiguity, which clearly has an important effect on the operation of an EEIG, will be resolved soon. It follows that the location of the official address should be considered carefully, as should the implications of applying the law of the country in which it is situated.

Changing the Address and the Law of the Grouping

The Regulation permits the official address of an existing Grouping to be changed from time to time within the original jurisdiction of registration and also for it to be transferred to another EC country, subject to going through a procedure to safeguard the interests of creditors before such change is effected. A decision to change the official address requires the Members' unanimous consent. Since it appears that a transfrontier change of official address will automatically precipitate a change in governing law of the Grouping, the desirability of making such change should be considered carefully.

Legal advice should be taken in relation both to national law (if any) subsequent to the Regulation and the general principles of law in the proposed jurisdiction to ascertain whether it is advisable for the Grouping to be made subject to the proposed law. Taxation advice should also be taken as to the consequences of such a change, not only on the Grouping, but also on each Member of the Grouping. It may be worth providing in the Formation Agreement that consequential amendments may be made to the Agreement to ensure that certain provisions will not take on a new meaning under any new applicable law.

When the transfer of the official address results in a change in the law applicable to the Grouping, a transfer proposal must be drawn up, filed and published in the same way as the original Formation Agreement. No decision to transfer may be taken for two months after the publication of the proposal. The transfer takes effect on the date on which the Grouping is registered at the registry for the new official address.

The Regulation provides that Member States may enact legislation to the effect that the transfer of an official address, which would result in a change of the law applicable, shall not take effect if within the two month period following the publication of the proposal, a competent authority in that Member State opposes it on grounds of public interest. The Statutory Instrument clothes the registrar with this power.

Some Relevant Local Law Matters

Among the matters left to be legislated by the national law of EC States in relation to the Regulation are the process for registration of an EEIG (including fees and penalties for failure to comply with registration requirements) and the maximum number of Members. Matters of general principle of foreign laws which may require research include:

(1) competition law;
(2) insolvency law;
(3) the meaning and effect of 'joint and several liability';
(4) limitation periods for actions brought against the Grouping and its Members;
(5) methods of assessing damages in claims against the Grouping and its Members;
(6) application of contingency fees; and
(7) whether there is any system for registration of charges over the assets of an EEIG in the country of registration in favour of a person registered or domiciled outside that country.

Taxation Considerations

While the principle for the taxation of Groupings is that the profits or losses resulting from the activities of a Grouping shall be taxable only in the hands of its Members, and not in the hands of the Grouping itself, it is understood that national tax laws will apply in every other way, particularly as regards the apportionment of profits, tax procedures and any obligations imposed by national tax law. Thus, when incorporating a Grouping in a particular country, or on the commencement of trade of a Grouping in a particular country, advice should be taken on the liability of the Grouping to pay VAT, payroll taxes, stamp duties, etc.

Since EEIGs are by definition international bodies, the Members of a Grouping should consider and take local and international tax advice on the consequences of their joining the Grouping, transferring assets into or out of the Grouping, taking any profits out of the Grouping, or bearing any of its losses or the tax consequences of any ultimate dissolution or winding up of the Grouping. Tax advice should also be taken on the activities to be undertaken by the Grouping and how these activities will be treated for tax purposes. For example, consideration should be given to the tax treatment of interest paid by and to the Grouping and royalties on intellectual property licensed by and to the Grouping.

Although it appears unlikely that any of the currently negotiated double tax treaties will apply to EEIGs themselves, the fact that Groupings will not be taxable on their profits means that double tax treaties between the various States where the Grouping carries on a trade and the State in which each Member is resident will need to be considered.

The taxation issues associated with a Grouping are dealt with in detail in Chapter 4.

Development of Local Law

As more EEIGs are formed, disputes will undoubtedly arise and be taken to court, and it will be necessary to investigate whether there are any judicial precedents relating to EEIGs in each proposed jurisdiction. It is clearly conceivable and, indeed, quite probable that differing jurisprudence and national laws will develop in relation to EEIGs in each EC State. However, since the interpretation of the Regulation lies chiefly within the jurisdiction of the European Court it is unlikely that the treatment of EEIGs will vastly differ from one Member State to another.

A comparison of such precedents and laws may lead to the conclusion that it is more favourable to incorporate and operate an EEIG in one EC State than any other. For instance, in the US, Delaware is the favourite State in which to incorporate as it has a favourable tax regime and simple and flexible rules for company incorporation.

It may also be that certain Member States, such as France, where a similar entity to the EEIG already exists, namely the Groupement d'Interet Economique (GIE), will apply to an EEIG the law applicable to that comparable legal personality. Indeed, in France, the GIE has been widely used and was the vehicle for the famous Airbus project and the French contractors' consortium digging the Channel Tunnel.

(2) Who May Set Up an EEIG?

Most Bodies and Legal Entities may Form an EEIG

The facility of an EEIG is widely available to natural persons operating in the EC, as well as companies and firms (including co-operative societies and other legal persons governed by public or private law) which have been formed in accordance with the law of a Member State and have their registered or statutory office and central administration in the EC. Throughout this chapter, the term 'person' shall include all such undertakings. The main criterion is that each of the Members of the EEIG should have been engaged in an 'economic activity' prior to the creation of the EEIG. The idea of 'economic activity' is to be interpreted in the widest sense.

The EEIG must have at least two Members, each from different EC countries and an EEIG incorporated in England and Wales may have any number of Members. An EEIG may not be a member of another EEIG (this is to avoid a complicated chain of liabilities in an international context) although there is no reason why in principle a person cannot be a Member of more than one EEIG.

Non-EC Companies and Persons

Companies, bodies and businesses set up or incorporated outside the EC may not directly participate in a Grouping. However, there is no reason why, for example, a Swiss or US company who already carried on an economic activity in the EC should not be able to participate indirectly in a Grouping by forming a subsidiary in a Member State, transferring its EC economic activity to its EC subsidiary and for such subsidiary to become a Member of the Grouping, provided its membership of the Grouping was ancillary to the purposes and business of such subsidiary and not the sole reason for its existence.

In practice, it is likely that successful Groupings will wish to admit Members indirectly from other countries outside the EC solely for reasons of economic necessity. It is easy to envisage that if a Grouping were set up, for example, for the purposes of sharing truck distribution facilities for a range of products which are sold and marketed throughout the whole of the European market, it would make little sense not to extend such an arrangement to EFTA countries such as Switzerland, Austria, Sweden, Norway and Finland and also Eastern Bloc countries if the products of such a truck distribution Grouping were to be sold in those non-EC countries.

Wider Groupings

While the provisions of the Regulation clearly envisage that the Grouping should have an 'EC essence', a practical watering down of such concept may arise in the case of individuals who wish to become Members of a Grouping. The Regulation states that for a natural person to be permitted to be a Member of a Grouping, he must carry on an industrial, commercial, craft or agricultural activity or provide professional or other services in the Community. The

Regulation does not seek to lay down the standard or intensity to which the commercial activity must be carried on in the Community. Standards used by taxing authorities for determining whether an entity will be liable for taxation in an EC State – such as the existence of a permanent establishment – will not necessarily be conclusive in determining whether a business satisfies the criteria of the Regulation to become a Member of a Grouping.

If the Grouping comprises only two natural persons those two persons must carry on their principal activities in the EC. There is no requirement for natural persons to be EC nationals. If, for example, a number of non-EC individuals trading principally from their home countries wished to become Members of an EEIG, they could do so with the aid of two natural persons having their principal activities in the EC or one such person and one company having its central administration there. This, however, would not be possible if those individuals joining from outside the EC carried on their trades in their home country through the medium of a private company which was not incorporated or had no subsidiary in the EC.

Number of Members

Although the number of Members in the Grouping may be limited by technical, marketing or geographical reasons, the number of Members that the Grouping will have should be considered from a practical standpoint of making the Grouping work. The structure of the Grouping is relatively flexible and when any fundamental changes are proposed to be made to it, decisions of Members have to be unanimous. Thus, if the Grouping is very large and one Member disagrees with a proposal, he may be able to frustrate the wishes of the other Members. This may leave the other Members with the choice of having either to wind up the Grouping, buy out the Member who has refused to concede on the point, or set up a new Grouping parallel with the old one, but on different terms.

However, the more Members in the Grouping, the greater will be the pool of capital and resources available to support the EEIG. Bearing in mind the joint and several liability of the Members, the larger the Grouping is, the lower the exposure of any one Member to claims by the Grouping's creditors.

Under the Regulation, Member States of the EC may limit the maximum number of Members to a number not less than 20. So far, no such legislation has been put in place. Certain Member States may have existing laws which will have a bearing on the ideal number of Members. For example, in France it is generally better not to create an EEIG with more than 300 Members because of a French fiscal rule which considers that where an organisation has more than 300 members, it is treated as taking subscriptions from the public which is prohibited pursuant to provisions of Art 23 of the Regulation.

(3) Fellow Members of the EEIG

Choosing Other Members

Every Member of an EEIG, whether they are the guiding light in setting up the EEIG or are being asked to join one, will want to choose fellow Members who, so far as possible, have appropriate skills and resources to fulfil the objects of the Grouping. It is undesirable for the Grouping to have one Member who is financially dominant over the Grouping, since that Member is likely to be the first one to be asked to meet the debts if the Grouping itself cannot pay; or alternatively if that member suffers a financial collapse, he is likely to bring down the other Members who may not be able to fund his share of the liabilities to the Grouping.

Groupings in expanding businesses will seek to choose parties who are going to have a like minded view and ability to expand along with the rest of the EEIG. Further, it will be preferable to try to find collaborators who have a similar attitude to business or who work in a similar business culture. There may be various other desired qualities of a business, financial or technical nature. Before joining a Grouping or admitting a new Member to a Grouping, every possible reasonable and practical check, visit or enquiry should be made in relation to the other Members of the Grouping.

Protection Against Other Members' Failure to Fulfil Obligations

Further and from a more legalistic standpoint, Members may want to have some legal recourse if other Members are unable to perform their respective duties and obligations under the Formation Agreement. The effectiveness and availability of such legal recourse will depend upon the proper law of the Formation Agreement applying at the relevant time.

Another factor to be borne in mind is how the taxation of an EEIG is to be treated in the country of which a proposed Member is a national. For example, UK tax law provides that in the case of a partnership, one partner will be personally liable for the other partners' tax debts arising out of profits or gains of the partnership. This rule was not applied generally to the whole European Community when adopting the Regulation, and remains merely as a national tax rule applicable in the UK. It will apply to any UK Member of a Grouping, irrespective of where such Grouping is incorporated. However, the Regulation provides that the Members will only be liable for the tax liabilities directly payable by the Grouping, for example, pay roll and turnover taxes. If a similar rule does not exist in a foreign Member's country, a UK Member should be aware that he may be liable to the UK for his foreign Member's tax debts, but such foreign Members may not be under a reciprocal liability for the UK Member's tax debts. A specific indemnity to cover this point should therefore be requested by a UK Member from the other Members.

Consequences of Other Members' Failure to Perform

In setting up, or joining a Grouping it is important for individual Members to consider carefully the ways in which they can protect themselves if any of the fundamental commercial or legal assumptions they have made about a fellow Member turn out to be incorrect. Members should consider whether to give and take any warranties to and from the other Members and, if so, what the consequences should be if any of those warranties are breached.

The reasons for giving warranties when forming a Grouping in a commercial context is to set out clearly the fundamental assumptions made – which may include some or all of the following:

(1) that all Members have legal capacity under the Regulation and any relevant national law to become Members of a Grouping;
(2) that no Member is prohibited by contract or any financial arrangements he has made, or through his professional body, or trade association or other law or legislation from fully participating in the Grouping's affairs in the manner in which the formation contract requires;
(3) that the Members have the financial, technical and managerial capacity to fulfil their obligations under the terms of the Formation Agreement.

Another reason for taking and giving warranties along with associated provisions is so that the parties can work out the consequences of any breach of warranty and if any matter is not capable of being resolved through amicable negotiation (which may be the case if a fundamental belief concerning a business partner has turned out to be untrue). If one Member cannot participate in the Grouping in the agreed manner and form, that Member may in practice be replaced with someone else who can; otherwise the venture may collapse, or be forced to continue with the other Members sharing a greater burden of responsibility within the Grouping. As a matter of law, the parties to a Formation Agreement need to decide whether a breach of warranty will allow non-breaching Members to claim damages against the breaching Member, to terminate the venture entirely, or to continue the venture without the breaching Member but to redistribute the costs and benefits in a pre-agreed adjusted manner among the remaining Members. If damages can be claimed against a defaulting and departing Member, or if costs and benefits may be redistributed among the remaining Members, thought should be given as to any tax loss that Members may incur as a consequence of the Member's departure. The proper place to address such issues is in the Formation Agreement, and these issues probably need to be discussed at an early stage of negotiations when forming a Grouping.

In considering whether such warranties should be given, it must be borne in mind that potential Members may be prohibited from Membership of an EEIG for a number of reasons. They may be restricted by:

(1) the Regulation, eg by virtue of being incorporated in a non-EC State; or
(2) contract, eg a restrictive covenant or covenant in a loan or investment agreement; or
(3) law, eg to join an EEIG may be contrary to a director's duty to a company, or a trustee's duty to his beneficiaries; or
(4) a Code of Practice or rule, eg a professional association may prohibit its members from becoming Members of an EEIG.

Problems of Mortgages or Charges Over Members' Assets or Undertakings

If a Member or proposed Member of the EEIG has given or proposes to give any general fixed or floating charge over his assets or undertaking (including his participation in the EEIG), this will operate in English law as an equitable assignment of the Member's participation as soon as he joins the Grouping. Under the Regulation an assignment is not permitted unless all the Members consent thereto, or the Formation Agreement provides otherwise. This point is addressed later in this chapter. Notice of any Member's assignment of his participation in the Grouping or a proportion thereof must be filed at the Companies Registry. Accordingly, prior to any person being admitted to membership of an EEIG, the existing Members should carry out searches at any mortgage or charges register in each relevant country to reveal any charges registered over the property of an incoming Member which would include any charge over the new Member's participation. Further, enquiries should be made of the incoming Member as to any relevant charges. A potential new Member may have to obtain a waiver or deed of release from his chargeholders prior to becoming a Member of the Grouping. Lawyers for the incoming Members should also enquire whether searches with regard to existing Members have been carried out with satisfactory results and where necessary such enquiries and disclosures should be repeated.

(4) How will the Grouping be Funded?

Flexible Funding Arrangements

The Regulation allows the Members of the Grouping a great deal of flexibility in funding the Grouping. Unlike a company, a Grouping does not necessarily require the Members to subscribe for an initial share capital. Obviously the

Grouping will require adequate funds to be provided to meet its liabilities and the Members will have a joint and several liability for the Grouping's debts.

The Grouping may in practice be funded in a variety of ways. The principal means will be:

(1) by the Members out of their own resources; or
(2) by external resources and secured on the assets of the Grouping and/or on the assets or covenants of the Members; or
(3) by the Members raising external funding on their own assets and/or covenanting and advancing such funding to the Grouping.

In each jurisdiction the tax effect of each funding method should be carefully considered with tax advisers.

They will now be discussed in turn more fully.

Members Funding the Grouping from their Own Resources

In order that it should be able to operate, the Members may fund the EEIG from their own resources as they wish. They may:

(a) place an initial seed capital into the Grouping;
(b) make monthly, quarterly or annual payments against budgeted expenses;
(c) provide loans to the Grouping;
(d) transfer to, or give the Grouping the right to use, certain assets (eg land, materials, plant, technology or know-how).

The tax consequences of actually transferring assets into a Grouping may be adverse. These may include the payment of stamp duty or other transfer taxes, a recapture of tax depreciation or capital allowances previously granted, or a disposal for capital gains tax purposes. Many of these consequences may be avoided in practice by not transferring the assets as such but merely making them available to the Grouping. The method by which this is achieved will of course depend on each individual set of circumstances. The simplest way of doing this, where there is no economic, legal or tax necessity for the Grouping itself to own the assets it needs to carry on its business, would be for the Members of the Grouping to lend, lease or license assets into the Grouping.

If asset transfers are to be made and are to be treated as part of the capital of the Grouping they should be valued so that disputes do not arise between the Members as to the extent of the contribution of the Member transferring such items into the Grouping. Another good reason for carefully valuing each Member's contribution is that if a Member becomes insolvent, his creditors will only have rights in relation to that Member's share of the assets of the Grouping.

The extent to which Members can, or should, fund a Grouping out of their own resources will depend on:

(a) the relevant needs of the Grouping;
(b) the financial strengths of the Members; and
(c) the purpose for which the Grouping was set up.

For example, if a French manufacturer of railway locomotives were to join a Grouping with two English banks to provide locomotives on contract hire to an English coal mining company, it might be that the project could be funded by the Members of the Grouping without recourse to outside funding, albeit that those Members finance the project in different ways. For example, the banks could provide tax based lease finance under a UK regime of writing down allowances, and the French manufacturer, who would not have access to UK writing down allowances, would provide training and maintenance services and back up locomotives to the English coal company. The overall object would be to further the business of both types of Members: the French locomotive manufacturer in supplying locomotives and the English banks in providing finance. Incidentally, under English law there is no prohibition against a bank being a Member of an EEIG. This example would not work if the lessor Member was French, since under French law a bank may not be a Member of an EEIG.

Funding for the Grouping from External Resources

Borrowings

There is nothing in the Regulation or the Statutory Instrument to prevent the Grouping being funded wholly or partly by bank borrowings or private placings of bonds or loan stock, if the Members feel that is appropriate. The Grouping can also, subject to the law of its country of incorporation, charge its assets and undertaking as security for any loan made to it. Any lender to a Grouping may require security not only over the Members' participations in the Grouping but additionally over other property of the Members. This will depend on the extent to which the Grouping can give the lender the security that it desires, on the nature of the financing and the strength of the financial covenants of the Members. In any event, the Members will be jointly and severally liable for the Grouping's borrowings, unless the lender agrees to waive its rights to claim in whole or in part from any Member. Whether Members of the Grouping, who are liable for taxation on the Grouping's profits, can obtain full allowance for tax purposes on borrowings incurred by the Grouping, is an issue which should be considered if major borrowings are to be made by the Grouping.

Project financing

Project financing is a term that describes an arrangement between the financiers of a project and the project vehicle, whereby the repayment of financial facilities is restricted to the earnings of the project itself. If the earnings of the project are insufficient to repay the financiers, the shareholders, Members or joint venturers in the project shall have no personal obligation to repay the financiers out of their own funds rather than the project's funds.

This method of financing could be used in any project where an EEIG is involved. One of the great strengths of an EEIG as a project finance vehicle is that it has legal personality and can enter into borrowing arrangements in its own right. Thus, if the financial covenant that the Grouping can offer to the lenders is sufficiently strong, there is no reason in principle why the lenders to the Grouping's project could not waive their rights against the Members of the Grouping to repay the borrowings if the Grouping failed to do so.

Off balance sheet financing

It is likely that in Great Britain it will not be necessary to consolidate the profits and losses arising in respect of a Grouping in the accounts of Member companies, although it may be necessary to enter a note in those accounts. This is a feature of a Grouping that may have attractions for structuring certain transactions. This subject is discussed in more detail in Chapter 4.

Security for borrowing and registration of charges

A Grouping can charge its assets and undertaking to secure a borrowing.

The provisions of Part XII of the Companies Act 1985 apply to EEIGs registered in England and Wales in relation to charges and registration. Therefore, a charge over land, wherever situated, a floating charge or charge on book debts, ships, aircraft, etc, created by an EEIG registered in England and Wales is void unless registered at Companies House. Further, although an EEIG registered outside England and Wales is under no duty to do so, it may submit particulars of a charge created over property in the UK for registration. The Registrar would refuse to register the charge but would note that particulars had been submitted for registration. This would give the EEIG limited protection by putting on notice anyone proposing to deal with the charged property that it was in fact the subject of a charge.

Under the Companies Act 1989, certain amendments are to be made to the current position. When the section relating to charges is put in force (which is expected to take place in March 1991) a charge over property, wherever situated, in favour of an EEIG registered outside Great Britain, but with an establishment in Great Britain, must be registered if it would require registration if created by a company registered in Great Britain. Further, those provisions of Part III of the Insolvency Act 1986 relating to the appointment of receivers and administrative receivers apply equally to EEIGs as to companies.

Members Raising External Financing and Advancing Funds to the Grouping

Many contractual joint ventures in the past have used this funding technique. A significant amount of North Sea Oil exploitation has used contractual joint ventures as a means of different companies combining together in an exploration activity. A great difficulty of the contractual joint venture has been that it does not have legal personality and therefore it is not in a position to borrow or raise funds in its own right. In such joint ventures, the Members have usually raised the funds in their own right and then advanced them to the joint venture.

The means whereby the Members can raise funds in their own right to advance to the Grouping are as wide as the capital and money markets can offer. The likelihood is that in practice the Member will borrow funds, raise equity from third parties (currently by way of private placing, venture capital or an issue of shares on a stock exchange) or procure leasing facilities from third parties to provide the Grouping with equipment. Any borrowings may be secured either on the assets of the Member generally or by way of a charge on his participation in the Grouping. If a Member takes a lease of equipment from a third party to lease it on subsequently to the Grouping, the Member must ensure he has power to sub-lease to the Grouping. If Members raise external funding and then advance it to the joint venture, the basis upon which such funds are advanced must be clearly agreed. The options available to the Members are (a) to treat the advance as a form of equity capital, earning a return only out of the rights of the Grouping, (b) to treat it as a non-recourse loan, being repaid only out of earnings of the venture, or (c) as a full recourse loan, repayable by the Grouping or the Members regardless of earnings or profits of the Grouping. This last treatment of such an advance is not likely to be very popular since one of the advantages of each Member being responsible for raising his own share of the funding is that the funding risk of the Grouping is compartmentalised ensuring that no Member of the Grouping becomes jointly and severally liable for the funding arrangements of any other Member.

Use of Participation as Security

The Regulation provides that a Member may only use his participation as security if all the other Members have given their consent, unless the Formation Agreement provides otherwise. The Regulation also states that a Member may only assign his participation if the other Members unanimously agree.

These two provisions are contradictory in the eyes of an English lawyer, since the giving of a security operates in English law by way of an equitable assignment. Until this ambiguity is resolved, it would appear advisable to allow for the giving of security over a Member's participation only if the other Members unanimously consent. As mentioned earlier, in the event of a conflict between the Regulation and national law, the former prevails. It follows that the giving or redeeming of a security in accordance with the national law, but in contravention of the Regulation, would be void.

In practice, a Member's participation in a Grouping is likely to be of limited value as security to a lender, since the lender may not step into the shoes of the Member and become a Member in his place without the unanimous consent of all the other Members of the Grouping. In the UK it is likely that the principal form of security which other Members of the Grouping would find it acceptable for a Member to grant will be limited to a charge over profit distributions or benefits deriving from the Grouping to each of its Members. Furthermore there is of course a great risk that Members may inadvertently breach the prohibition (that they shall not charge their interest in the Grouping without their fellow Members' consent) if they are asked by their bankers or other lenders to give a general charge over their assets and undertaking, since in doing so they may grant a charge over their participation. This should be considered carefully by the managers and Members of the Grouping at the outset, when investigating new Members and also during the life of any Grouping.

Consequences of Members Failing to Fund their Share of Liabilities

There are two particular eventualities that need to be catered for if a Member fails to meet his share of liabilities. The first of these occurs when a Member fails to pay his share of funding to the Grouping, eg where it has been agreed that the Grouping shall be funded by the Members making quarterly contributions to the Grouping's expenses against a budget and one Member fails to pay his contribution on time or at all. The second is where the Grouping incurs an unexpected and unbudgeted liability that it cannot meet out of its own funds for which the Members are jointly and severally liable.

In the first case, where the Member fails to make his contribution, the options are:

(1) to terminate the project, if that is possible;
(2) to expel the Member, subject to the others having a claim against it for its unpaid contribution;
(3) to allow it to remain a Member in a reduced capacity, either by adjusting its share amongst the other Members if there is only a partial shortfall in contributions; or placing it in the category of defaulting Member, who as such has no entitlement to any share of benefits or profits of the Grouping or to any return of its capital introduced into the Grouping until such time as the project of the Grouping has become cash positive and the other Members have had their capital returned.

In the second case, the problem may be difficult since it is likely that the financial burden suddenly placed on the Grouping and its Members will be very heavy. If the burden is too heavy it may be necessary to wind up the Grouping.

However, if the burden can be carried by the other Members then they must rely on their rights to claim an indemnity against the defaulting Member (for what that may be worth). Whatever the eventuality being provided for and whichever course of remedial action is adopted, the Formation Agreement must clearly set out the consequences of a Member's failure to fulfil his obligations to the Grouping.

(5) What Provisions should the Formation Agreement Contain?

Having decided where and with whom to form a Grouping, the next step is the preparation of the Formation Agreement. The Formation Agreement may either come into operation immediately, although the Grouping will not acquire legal personality and be able to enter into contracts with others until it has been registered, or the contract or certain parts of it may only come into effect conditionally upon certain events occurring.

Conditional Formation Agreements

The circumstances in which Members will choose to proceed to set up a Grouping may vary. One or more of the Members may need to adjust their affairs or secure some contract before entering into the Grouping. The viability of the Grouping's venture may be conditional on such matters occurring. If, however, all the other aspects of the venture in the terms of the Formation Agreement have been agreed, it may be appropriate to draft the Formation Agreement on a conditional basis so as to provide that as soon as the necessary conditions have been satisfied the incorporation will proceed. For example, formation of a Grouping could be made conditional upon a loan facility from a bank being made available.

Having decided when the Formation Agreement is going to take effect, the Members can move on to agree matters required by the Regulation.

Name of the Grouping

The parties need to decide on the name the Grouping will have, since the Regulation requires each Grouping to have a name which is duly registered.

In England and Wales, the name must not include any of the following words: 'Membership', 'unlimited' or 'public limited company' or their Welsh equivalents. The Registrar of Companies at Companies House has certain powers to reject the name of an EEIG which is too similar to the name of another company or EEIG registered in England and Wales. Furthermore, an EEIG will be subject to the same rules as any other legal entity relating to business or trade names and the law of passing off or infringement of trademarks or service marks, namely that no business may have a name which is too similar to an existing business name in which another business has established rights, either through long use or registration. Other Member States apply similar restrictions. Therefore, before the EEIG is formed, trade and service mark and business and company name searches should be carried out in each and every jurisdiction where it is intended that the EEIG should carry on business or be registered as having an establishment.

Since an EEIG by definition is an international entity, this exercise will require not just a consideration of the results of such searches against the background of laws relating to business names in each relevant country, but also a consideration of the meaning and connotations of the relevant name in each country of use. The choice of an inappropriate name for the EEIG could give rise to dire and embarrassing consequences.

Parties considering forming a Grouping should not underestimate the time that may need to be taken in choosing and finding a name that is available and culturally suitable in several different jurisdictions. Name searches and enquiries should be put in hand at the earliest opportunity.

Official Address

Parties forming the Grouping must decide on the official address to be adopted by the Grouping. Such address must be stated in the Formation Agreement. The official address must be situate in the European Community and must be either:

(1) where the group has its central administration; or
(2) where one of the Members of the Grouping has its central administration or, in the case of a natural person, his principal activity, provided that the Grouping carries on an activity from the same premises.

Since there is a need for the official address to coincide with real activity carried on by the Grouping, it is unlikely that the current practice of many UK companies to have their registered offices with their lawyers or accountants will occur in the case of EEIGs.

As previously mentioned, it is understood that the draughtsmen of the Regulation intended the jurisdiction in which the official address is situated to determine the law governing the Grouping and a transnational change in the official address will affect a change in the law of the Grouping.

Objects of the Grouping

The Formation Agreement should state the objects for which the Grouping is formed. A discussion about the proposed objects of the Grouping will probably result in several other points coming to light, all of which will need careful consideration.

The Regulation permits an EEIG to have a very wide range of objects to carry out almost any form of activity. However, the objects must be related to and based on the economic activities of its Members. An EEIG is intended to enable its Members, by pooling their activities, resources or services, to develop their own economic activities. Its purpose should not be to make profits for itself, though it is not prohibited from making profits. Such profits will be treated as being attributed to its Members for tax purposes in accordance with each Member's profit sharing ratio.

An EEIG should not be used as a vehicle to carry out a new activity which has no connection with the activities of its Members, nor must it replace the economic activities of its Members, nor become so important that their activities are taken over by it or become dependent upon it. The activities of the Grouping must therefore be ancillary to those of its Members. It may be that certain successful Groupings will in time have to become companies because they will become businesses in their own right and not accessories to the businesses of their Members. Within these limitations the EEIG may undertake activities in a multitude of fields and over time the objects of the EEIG can be scaled up or down depending on how the participation and co-operation of the Members develop.

Certain objects, however, are prohibited, such as exercising, directly or indirectly, a power of management or supervision over the activities of its Members or another undertaking, particularly in the fields of personnel, finance and investment. It would appear that these prohibitions are not intended to be interpreted too strictly. At first sight, they would appear to rule out Groupings whose objects were to train staff for Members of the Grouping or to invest surplus cash generated by Members of the Grouping. However, it might be possible to achieve such ends as training, if the objects approved were widely drafted so as to provide that it would make available such resources as the Members required, so that in practice the employees in training would become employees of the Grouping, rather than of the Members, and the Grouping could be given the power to train its own employees. It should be noted, however, that the Regulation prohibits a Grouping from having more than 500 employees.

Quite apart from the provisions of the Regulation in relation to the objects of a Grouping, expert legal advice should be taken in Member States in which it is intended to operate to ascertain whether any national laws may restrict the objects. For example, a Grouping could not act in France as a bank because that can only be done by a public or private company and then only under strict conditions.

Further, the EEIG may not directly or indirectly hold shares of any kind in a Member undertaking and may only hold shares in another undertaking if it is necessary for the achievement of the Grouping's objects and if it is done on the Members' behalf.

Since it is the intention that a Grouping should only be ancillary to the activities of its Members, it is not entitled to offer participations, loan notes or shares to the public.

It should also be noted that a Grouping should not be used by a company for such purposes as making loans to directors or as a vehicle through which to transfer property from directors to companies for whom they work, when such activities are contrary to the provisions of English company law or the International Stock Exchange Regulations.

Methods for Achieving the Grouping's Objects

Even if the objects of the Grouping have been determined, the means of achieving them must be worked out, not just in a practical sense but also in terms of their economic and tax implications.

For example if the Grouping were formed with the intention of marketing and distributing goods produced by the Members it would have the option of either acting as a principal or acting as an agent. If the Grouping acted as a 'principal' it would purchase the goods from each Member, sell, package, deliver invoices for the goods and collect the proceeds of sale on its own behalf, at the end of the year making a distribution of profits to its Members. If it acted solely as an 'agent' for each of the Members it would provide a packaging, selling, delivering, invoicing service to its Members *at cost*. As the concept of the EEIG was designed essentially for sharing costs rather than for sharing or limiting risks, or for making profits, the 'agency' rather than the 'principal' method of operation of a Grouping is likely to be more appropriate.

If the 'agency' method of operation is adopted, then the cost of capitalising the business remains with each of the Members to the extent that they use the Grouping's services, as the risk of bad debts on sales of goods remains with each Member and does not have to be shared with each of the other Members under the principle of joint and several liability. If the Grouping only operates with the intention of sharing costs (and not making profits out of trading as a principal), the issue of the Members paying tax on profits of the Grouping is avoided (unless any relevant tax authority requires the Grouping to make some minimal profit by setting its prices to its Members at, eg cost plus ten per cent, in which case the issue of paying tax on the profits of the Grouping is minimized) and a Member need only ensure, from a tax standpoint:

(1) that the costs charged by the Grouping to him are effectively treated as deductible costs of the Members' business in computing the profits of that business; and
(2) that he receives the benefit of any income generated on his behalf by the agent Grouping.

Property of the Grouping

Consideration of the objects of an EEIG and the means of achieving those objects must be with a clear view as to what property the Grouping will own, ie whether it is land, intellectual property and knowhow, contracts, plant, equipment, etc.

Thus, if a group of haulage companies operating similar trucks throughout Europe wished to reduce their overall holding of expensive spare parts in countries away from their home base while maintaining easy access to such spares, they might form an EEIG to manage the pooling of their spare parts. This could be done in a variety of ways, for example, either the EEIG could act as a central purchasing body for all spare parts which it would then store and sell to Members as and when and where they were needed, or, alternatively, the EEIG could act solely as an administrator and clearing house for the distribution and exchange of spare parts which however, would continue to be owned, located and warehoused by each individual Member.

Equally, if an EEIG were to be formed to promote and distribute a range of craft products in the European Market under the trade name of, eg 'Eurocraft', who would own that trademark? Would the EEIG own the mark and license all Members to use it for the sale of their craft work, or would one or more of the Members own the mark and license the Grouping and the other Members to use it for distributing particular products?

It is usually appropriate for such matters to be dealt with in some detail in the Formation Agreement, including provisions for regular valuing of the property of the Grouping. It should also be set out clearly whether goodwill created in the Grouping is to be owned by the Grouping itself or by the Members.

The ownership of property by a Grouping is likely to give rise to capital and transfer tax issues. Members' shares of property, whether specific or generally owned by a Grouping, will be determined for tax purposes by reference to the Formation Agreement. If no asset sharing ratios are specified, profit sharing ratios will be used. If these are not set out in the Formation Agreement, it will be presumed that assets and profits will be shared equally. In appropriate circumstances it may be possible for Members to avoid paying capital gains taxes, stamp duty and other transfer taxes on transferring assets into the Grouping, by the relevant Member leasing, lending or licensing them to the Grouping.

Benefits and Restrictions upon Members

Another issue which must be determined when considering the objects of the Grouping is the extent to which the Members of the Grouping may be entitled to receive benefits and be obliged to enter into certain restrictions in order for those objects to be achieved. This point may be best illustrated through a couple of examples.

Equal entitlement to benefits

If a group of paint manufacturers were to enter into a Grouping for the purpose of carrying out joint research into new paint products, then it would be essential to each Member that they were all simultaneously entitled to receive the results of such research and they were all entitled to receive research findings of the same depth and quality so that no Member was favoured by the Grouping in relation to the benefits of the research.

Unequal entitlement to benefits

When forming a Grouping which is likely to own assets of any worth or assets that may appreciate or depreciate, it may be sensible to spell out the asset sharing ratio. This would allow individual Members to know what share of liability they may have for Capital Gains Tax on assets sold at a profit and what capital or depreciation allowances they may be able to claim. This would be particularly relevant to a Member who transferred assets into a Grouping and was concerned about the claw back or loss of previously claimed depreciation or writing down allowances. For example, a Member who had previously purchased assets and claimed depreciation allowances on them, who transferred them to a Grouping in which he had a one-fifth share of the assets and no other Members transferred any assets to the Grouping, should then suffer a claw back of the depreciation allowance he had been given, and would only be able to claim a new depreciation allowance on his one-fifth share of the assets in the Grouping. If, however, the Formation Agreement provided that he was to be treated as the only Member of the Grouping having a share in the specific assets that he had transferred into the Grouping, he might then find that, while he may have suffered a claw back of depreciation allowances already given to him when he held the assets for use in his own business, he could nevertheless claim a new depreciation allowance on the value of all the assets he had transferred into the Grouping.

Commitment to support activity

In other circumstances, in order to make the venture worthwhile, it may be necessary for each Member to undertake to place a certain amount of a specific type of business with the Grouping. Thus, if a group of chemical companies were to collaborate to build a toxic waste incinerator to dispose of a particular type of toxic waste that they all produced, it may be necessary for Members of the Grouping to enter into some form of 'take or pay' agreement with the Grouping, whereby even if they did not take up their allotted use of the facility, they would nevertheless have to pay for it as if they had used it.

Restrictions

It may sometimes be necessary for the Members to enter into some form of agreement not to compete with the Grouping. If it is agreed that as between the Members certain activities previously carried on by each of them should come within the exclusive province of the Grouping, it may be necessary to provide in the Formation Agreement that the Members will account to the Grouping for any benefits and profits they may make or achieve on their own in competition with the Grouping.

An EEIG is not exempt from either EC or national competition law. It follows that all agreements between Members relating to the objects of the Grouping, the benefits to be received and the restrictions, if any, to be undertaken, should be carefully considered to see that they do not have the effect of infringing EC or national competition law of the countries of the registered office or principal activity of any of the Members, or places of operation of the Grouping. If it is likely that the entering into of restrictions by Members will so infringe, Members forming a Grouping should consider taking competition law advice in each relevant jurisdiction before forming a Grouping and in particular before the Members of the Grouping, whether in the Formation Agreement or otherwise, enter into restrictions on competition between themselves. (See the discussion of competition law towards the end of this Chapter, p 66.)

Joint and Several Liability

When considering the objects of the Grouping another issue which needs to be addressed is what the effects of the objects of the Grouping will be on the joint and several liability of the Members. The Regulation provides that, while each Grouping is a legal entity in its own right, the Members of the Grouping will be jointly and severally liable for the debts and liabilities of the Grouping.

Members in practice will only actually be liable for the Grouping's debts insofar as it is shown that the liability was properly incurred by the Grouping and then not until a creditor has requested the Grouping to pay and it has failed to do so within a reasonable period of time.

Any such liability will continue for a period of five years after a Member leaves the Grouping. The imposition of joint and several liability by the Regulation is a consequence of the Regulation not requiring the Grouping to have to maintain a minimum capital, and therefore there may be no central fund as such and creditors of the Grouping may not receive any financial guarantee. The real degree of risk that any one of the Members actually runs of any creditors making a claim against him depends on the extent to which the Members have 'capitalised' the Grouping or otherwise properly funded it, through the transfer of property to the Grouping or by making regular contributions to its expenses.

The counterbalance to joint and several liability is that any Member has a right to an indemnity from the other Members if he is made to pick up a bill of the Grouping. That right to an indemnity however, may be of little practical value if the other Members of the Grouping do not have the resources to meet their share of the liability.

Limitation of Liability

In practice, there may well be an element of 'deep pocket syndrome' applying to claims made against the Members of the EEIG, in that creditors will tend to press their claims against the more wealthy participants of the Grouping. In order to reduce this risk and the amount of the total 'pool' of capital available to creditors of the Grouping, it may be appropriate for companies which are considering becoming Members of an EEIG to do so through an EC subsidiary company which is capitalised at a level that they feel is appropriate to fund their stake in the EEIG and to perform their obligations. The level at which such intermediary subsidiary company shall be capitalised or otherwise funded must be agreed in advance by the Members of the Grouping. If the Member of the EEIG is a subsidiary company then it must comply with the requirements of the Regulation as to who may be a Member, set out above. In order to do so, it will be necessary for some part of the business and undertaking of the parent company relating to its operation in the EC to be transferred to its EC subsidiary. The use of such a corporate Membership structure may be particularly appropriate where the objects and activities of the Grouping are of a potentially high risk nature.

Ratio of Funding

The Members of an EEIG are free to decide how to fund the Grouping in any manner or proportion. In the absence of such provision in the Formation Agreement or other written Agreement the Members will be required to contribute in equal shares. The provisions of the Formation Agreement dealing with the funding ratio will need to be looked at carefully, especially where it has been agreed that one or more Members, for tax or other reasons, will not transfer capital or revenue sums into the Grouping, but will just make certain assets available to the Grouping.

Sharing of Profits and Losses

As financial obligations in the Formation Agreement are one of the matters most likely to give rise to arguments amongst the Members, it is wise to set out those financial obligations as clearly as possible at the outset. The agreement should spell out the basis for sharing the future profits and losses while the Members all remain Members of the Grouping. The principles should be set out upon which any Member leaving, retiring or being expelled from the Grouping may have any capital contribution refunded to him and how any profits or losses of the Grouping at that time or arising thereafter will be shared. The mechanics of valuation of such payments can and should also be dealt with in the Formation Agreement. However, it is not permitted under the Regulation to attach an absolute value to the rights and obligations of a Member on leaving the Grouping, in advance of that event happening. Such rights and obligations must be calculated taking into account the assets and liabilities of the Grouping as they stand when the Member ceases to belong to it.

Inspection of Books and Records

Although the Regulation entitles Members to obtain information from managers concerning the Grouping's business and to inspect the Grouping's books and business records, it may be desirable to give in the Formation Agreement more specific powers of inspection of the Grouping's books and accounts and to obtain copies of the same.

Admission of New Members

As the structure of a Grouping may need to change over time, parties initially forming the Grouping should decide at the outset how new Members should be admitted and on what terms. It is probably appropriate to decide whether the admission of a new Member will require the unanimous approval of existing Members, although in practice this will almost always be the case. It is also sensible to provide in the original Formation Agreement that any new Member will give warranties to the existing Members in the same terms as the existing Members gave warranties to each other as to their legal, financial and technical capacity to enter into the agreement and perform their obligations, and also to set out what the consequences will be if the new Member breaches such warranties.

Cessation of Membership

Even if the Members can reach agreement as to how the Grouping should be set up, they may only have agreed for the Grouping to exist for a period of time or to carry out one particular project that is limited in time. If so, that limitation or cessation of Membership should be clearly set out in the Formation Agreement.

Voluntary cessation

It may transpire from time to time that Members may wish to leave the Grouping or a majority of Members may wish one of the Members to withdraw. In most circumstances this is likely to be an emotive issue and therefore it is probably better to make clear from the beginning in the Formation Agreement when Members may withdraw and on what terms. Unless this is set out in the Formation Agreement, the Regulation provides that Members may only withdraw with the unanimous consent of all the other Members or on 'just and proper grounds'.

Compulsory cessation

It may be desired that individual Members are compelled to retire upon attaining the statutory retirement age in any one of the jurisdictions in which the Grouping is operating, although this is not a matter required by the Regulation. The Regulation provides that any Members of a Grouping may be expelled for the reasons listed in the Formation Agreement and in any case if he seriously fails in his obligations or if he causes or threatens to cause serious disruption in the operation of the Grouping. The Members may therefore wish to state specific circumstances in which a Member may be forced to leave the Grouping, eg if he fails to attend meetings of the Members, if he becomes insolvent, etc. The Members should also consider if such unfortunate circumstances arise, whether expulsion should be automatic or should require the consent of all the other Members or at least a majority of them. If the Formation Agreement is silent on this point, expulsion may occur only by the decision of a court to which joint application has been made by a majority of the other Members.

Death of Members

If the Grouping is to include any individuals, in the event of the death of the individual Member no person may become a Member in his place except under any conditions laid down in the Formation Agreement, or, failing that, with the unanimous agreement of the remaining Members. The Members should therefore agree at the outset in the Formation Agreement what they intend to happen if one of them dies.

Continuing Obligations of Outgoing Members

Great care should be taken in determining what restrictive covenants, if any, should be imposed upon an outgoing Member, particularly since the objects of the Grouping will of necessity be related to and based on the economic activities of its Members. Advice should be taken from local lawyers in all relevant jurisdictions as to the validity, enforceability and registration requirements for restrictions to ensure that the intentions of those setting up the EEIG may be put into practice and that a member who has voluntarily left or been expelled may be prohibited from attacking the Grouping which he has just left.

The Regulation also provides for a period of five years for limitations of actions against an outgoing Member. Under English law, the period of limitation in contract is either six or 12 years, depending upon the circumstances. It therefore follows that in Great Britain there will be a period during which the outgoing Member is released from any liability to the other Members, but the remaining Members will remain liable. It may in certain circumstances be desirable for bank bonds or insurance policies to be taken out to cover claims brought in respect of that interim period.

Effect on Remaining Members

The Formation Agreement should clearly state whether the Grouping will continue to exist for the remaining Members after a Member has ceased to belong to it, or whether it will be dissolved. The Regulation provides that in the absence of such a provision, the Grouping will continue to exist. Provided the economic purpose of the Grouping can and does survive the departure of a Member, it is probably appropriate to draft the Formation Agreement on the assumption that the voting rights and participations of and profit sharing ratios of the remaining Members will be adjusted proportionately if an outgoing Member is not replaced, or is replaced by a new Member having different rights from those of the outgoing Member. It should be recalled that a Member leaving or joining a Grouping, or a change of asset sharing ratios, will give rise to the acquisition or disposal of assets in the Grouping between Members which may give rise to charges to Capital Gains Tax.

Transfer of Membership

The Regulation provides that a Member's participation shall not be assigned without the unanimous consent of the other Members and that the parties cannot contract out of this obligation in their Formation Agreement. If the assignment is by way of giving a security over the participation, it appears that the unanimous consent of the other Members will be required (see Problems of Mortgages and Charges, at p 40). If the form of transfer of the participation releases the new Member from liability for obligations arising prior to his admission, this provision may only be relied upon against third parties if it is notified to the Registrar and thereby made public. In drafting the provisions of the Formation Agreement it may also be worth including a clause relating to pre-emption rights on transfer so that an outgoing Member is first obliged to offer his participation in the Grouping to each of the other Members in direct proportion to their interests in the Grouping so that the remaining Members either take absolutely or until such time as a third party can be brought in from outside to take the participation of the outgoing Member. To a limited extent, this gives a further degree of control over who may become a Member of the Grouping.

Filing of Documents on Members Joining or Leaving an EEIG

On Members joining or leaving an EEIG, the managers must ensure that the necessary forms in each relevant country where the Grouping is registered or carries on business, are filed with the appropriate Registry in that country. It may also be necessary for changes to Membership to be advertised in the various national official gazettes.

Management

Two Controlling Groups

The Regulation provides that a Grouping should comprise of two controlling or managing groups:

(a) Members, who in many ways have a similar role to shareholders in a company; and
(b) managers, who carry out a similar role to company directors.

It is open to the Members (within certain limits) in their Formation Agreement to set out how the powers and duties of Members and managers should inter-relate and how decisions of the management should be taken. Ultimately, however, the Members are always the decision-making body of the Grouping and the managers carry out the Grouping's day-to-day activities. There are no requirements for regular consultation, for the holding of annual general meetings of Members or for holding monthly 'board meetings' of managers, although it is open to the managers or any Member of the Grouping to request all the Members be consulted in respect of any issue affecting the Grouping.

Appointment of managers

The Regulation provides that a Grouping shall be managed by one or more natural persons appointed in the Formation Agreement or by a decision of the Members. Neither the Regulation nor the Statutory Instrument legislates in detail how such appointment is to be made. Indeed, the Regulation specifically leaves the conditions for the appointment and removal of the managers and the laying down of their powers to be determined by the Formation Agreement or, failing that, by a unanimous decision by the Members. It may be that in practice each Member will wish to appoint a manager, thereby ensuring there is at least one manager appointed in each country in which a Member resides.

Managers to be persons or companies

In Great Britain a manager may be either an individual or a company, provided, if it is a company, that it designates one or more natural persons to represent it and notice of particulars of each such person is sent to the Registrar of Companies as though he were a manager. Anyone designated under this heading is subject to the same liabilities as though he were himself a manager. A manager need not necessarily be a Member.

Joint managers

The Regulation provides that the Formation Agreement may stipulate that a Grouping shall be validly bound by two or more managers acting jointly. Such a clause may only be relied upon against third parties if it is notified to the Registrar of Companies and published in the Official Gazette. If no express provision is included in the Formation Agreement, a single manager may bind the Grouping and cause the Members to be jointly and severally liable for his acts. Any third party dealing with the Grouping need not concern himself with what restrictions the Members and the Grouping have sought to impose on the manager to curb his powers, since such limitations as between themselves do not affect a third party.

Managers' service contracts

In drafting the Formation Agreement, it is probably appropriate for provisions to be inserted dealing with:

(a) the managers;
(b) their powers;
(c) any restrictions on their powers;
(d) their duties and any rights applying to them;
(e) the terms upon which managers will be appointed and permitted to retire.

It may be advisable to enter into separate service contracts between the managers and the Grouping. This would save the Formation Agreement becoming excessively complicated.

Managers' powers and duties

The Formation Agreement should stipulate between the Members how many managers will be appointed and on what terms. Members should consider what the managers' duties are to be, such as:

(i) to procure the registration of the Grouping;
(ii) to keep full and proper accounts and to provide management and annual accounts to Members;
(iii) the appointment of auditors;
(iv) the preparation of budgets.

Managers should probably be enpowered to:

(v) employ staff;
(vi) call meetings;
(vii) manage and conduct the affairs of the Grouping on a day-to-day basis;
(viii) pay expenses;
(ix) exercise any powers of the Grouping that are not required to be exercised by the Members.

Furthermore, if internally it is felt that there should be any restrictions on the managers' powers to enter into contracts of a particular size, or as to when one or more signatures are required on a contract, or on a bank account, such provisions should probably be set out. For the sake of good order and housekeeping, it is probably appropriate to consider setting out some legal duties which will apply to a manager, such as the duty of skill and care with which he shall perform his job, the fact that he should disclose any interest in contracts of which the Grouping is a party, and should, where possible, avoid entering into any conflict of interest between his position as a manager and his self interest. As the guardian of the day-to-day affairs of the Grouping, it may be appropriate to impose upon the manager a duty not to permit the group to trade while it is insolvent.

Managers' remuneration

As mentioned above, it may be appropriate for the Grouping to enter into a separate contract with each manager that sets out these provisions in further detail. Such a contract should also stipulate:

(i) the terms upon which he will be remunerated;
(ii) whether his salary will be varied;
(iii) whether he will receive any benefits such as life insurance, a pension, or use of a motor car, etc;
(iv) any restrictions applicable to him;
(v) the legal duties he is expected to satisfy and perform in his capacity as a manager.

Provision may also be made as to the circumstances in which he can retire, whether at national retiring age, at some other age or date, whether through incapacity or otherwise. Obviously the terms upon which a manager is engaged will depend on whether he is a full time professional manager retained to run the Grouping or whether he is in fact one of the Members or a representative of one of the Members and only carrying out a part time managerial activity.

Meetings of Members and Decision Making

It is entirely a matter for the Members to decide how, where and when to meet. If the Grouping is to comprise more than a few Members, it may be sensible to consider the provisions concerning meeting and decision making in some detail and the following matters may be significant.

The Regulation lays down certain essential provisions that must apply to the decision-making process of the Grouping and accordingly, in the absence of agreement to the contrary between the Members in the Formation Agreement, each Member shall have one vote. If the Formation Agreement, however, permits certain Members to have more than one vote, no Member may control a majority of the votes for the Grouping. Also certain fundamental decisions which would be capable of changing the foundations of the Grouping must be taken unanimously by the Members. Furthermore, other decisions not requiring unanimity by the Members may be taken by a majority provided the percentage of majority and the circumstances for the majority decision are set out in the Formation Agreement.

If the Members agree that meetings should have a chairman they must decide who should be the chairman and what should be his role, eg whether he shall have power to adjourn meetings and whether he is to have any casting vote in the case of any equality of votes. So far as the calling of meetings is concerned, while the Regulation provides that Members and managers may call meetings, it is probably appropriate to provide that the meeting will take place within a fairly limited period of time after its request so that matters needing to be discussed can be done so promptly.

Since the Members will often be in different countries, it is probably sensible to agree where meetings will take place and whether it will be necessary to travel or whether meetings may be held by telephone or video link. If meetings are to consider substantive issues, Members may require two or three weeks' notice of the meetings and their agenda so as to prepare for them. The parties should decide what form of quorum they require for the various meetings. Obviously, where a meeting requires unanimity, the quorum will have to be all the Members. However, if the matter is to be decided only by a majority voting, not all the Members need be present to form a quorum. Members should also incorporate in the Formation Agreement exactly how votes will be taken; whether by way of a show of hands or on some form of poll, whether persons can appoint proxies, etc. It should also be stipulated whether Members wish to have at least an annual general meeting or take records of meetings to provide and circulate minutes.

All such provisions concerning meetings are likely to be fairly lengthy in the Formation Agreement. A short-form method of achieving the same end may be to incorporate certain parts of Table A of the Companies Act 1985, amended so that its terminology applies to an EEIG. In order that the Members can be informed, all Members should have an express right set out in the Formation Agreement that the Grouping will provide them with such accounting and other information as they shall request and the managers should have imposed upon them a duty to see that the Grouping complies with such obligations.

Accounting and Taxation Matters

While these subjects are dealt with in greater length in Chapter 4 of this book, matters which need to be considered at the time of formation include:

(1) the currency in which the Grouping's accounts are to be prepared and in which currency transactions between Members and the Grouping shall be made;
(2) whether interest should be paid on overdrawn accounts of Members;
(3) who the auditors should be and how they may be removed;
(4) whether the Members must consider the accounts at an annual meeting;
(5) in what form the accounts will be prepared, to what accounting standards and with what frequency;
(6) when the financial year of the Grouping is to run from and to.

Since the Grouping may be operating in a number of different countries in different currencies, and indebtedness between the Members and the Grouping may have to be settled in a currency other than the principal currency of any Member, a Member settling any payment to the Grouping in a currency other than in the officially recognised currency of the Grouping may expose himself to an exchange risk. This might be minimised by the Members agreeing that the accounts and liabilities of the Grouping be settled in ECUs. Such exposures may be reduced by taking practical steps such as purchasing swaps or options for foreign currency. Equally, financial settlements made in a currency other than the principal one of the Grouping may similarly give rise to exchange risks. In this case a currency indemnity should be sought from the other party dealing with the Grouping.

At the time of writing, most EC countries have not finalised their rules on the tax liabilities of Groupings for such matters as the PAYE and VAT that Groupings will have to pay, so it is not possible to say if any particular provisions will need to be included in the Formation Agreement. In principle, it would appear that tax liabilities of the Grouping in each country in which it operates should be treated as a cost of operation to be borne by the Members of the Grouping. Any tax and national insurance contributions debts incurred by a Grouping in the UK would be recoverable only against UK assets. By contrast, VAT debts can be recovered in other Member States. In order for Members to be certain that they can receive an indemnity for liabilities incurred in another jurisdiction but not enforceable in their own, it may be worthwhile inserting an express indemnity provision in the Formation Agreement to cover this point.

Since taxation of profits of the Grouping is to be carried out at the level of the Members, not at the level of the Grouping, it would not seem to be necessary for the Formation Agreement to include any particular provisions other than those referred to specifically in this chapter and in Chapter 4. Relevant national tax law will apply to each Member and the apportionment of profits and the taxation of profits as between different Members should be dealt with pursuant to the rules of the double tax agreements applying between the various Member States.

Winding Up

The Regulation provides that a decision to wind up the Grouping shall be taken unanimously by the Members unless the Formation Agreement provides otherwise. This is a point which should be carefully considered by the Members in drafting the Formation Agreement. The Regulation also provides that in certain circumstances the Grouping must be wound up, ie where the Grouping was formed only for a fixed period which has expired, or was formed to accomplish a specific purpose which it is either not possible to achieve, or which has been achieved. If such circumstances occur, and the Members do not decide to wind up the Grouping within three months, any Member may petition the court to order winding up. Also, in the event of the Grouping becoming insolvent, a creditor may petition the Grouping to be wound up.

The law governing the insolvency of an EEIG is the law of each relevant Member State. Thus, a Grouping registered in England and Wales could be wound up in the event of insolvency in any other EC Member State. Under the law of England and Wales it would appear that Groupings can only be wound up (whether due to reasons of insolvency or otherwise) by making an application to court for the winding up as if the Grouping were an overseas company. This, however, does not appear to be the intention of the Regulation and some changes to the Statutory Instrument may be required.

Nullity

The Formation Agreement may be declared void by a judicial decision. Once a Grouping is declared void, it must be wound up, and the judgment must be published in the Gazette and the Official Journal. Where a third party acts in good faith with the Grouping, unaware of its nullity, then the Grouping can only rely on the nullity as from the date of such advertisement in both publications.

Jurisdiction and Service

To provide in advance for any dispute arising between the parties, it is advisable to include a clause to say that the courts of the country whose law governs the Formation Agreement and the operation of the Grouping shall have non-exclusive jurisdiction to deal with any disputes. The procedure for service of legal proceedings instigated in one Member State on persons in other Member States has been significantly simplified by the 1968 Convention on Jurisdiction and Judgments. This Convention was enacted in English law by the Civil Jurisdiction and Judgments Act 1982. However, methods of serving documents are subject to different formalities in different Member States and are sometimes subject to conventions and agreements concluded between Member States which often require official channels to be used. In order to avoid these formalities, it may be simpler for all non-British Members to be required in the Formation Agreement to specify the name and address of a reliable person in England and Wales to accept service of proceedings on his behalf, even though such a provision may seem unusual to non-British persons.

Method of Dispute Resolution

While the parties can leave the resolution of any disputes to the courts, it is open to the parties to choose any other means of dispute resolution, such as conciliation (with the help of an expert if necessary) or arbitration, or a mixture of conciliation, arbitration and legal proceedings.

Notices and Time Stipulation

Since the EEIG Formation Agreement will operate as an agreement between various persons in different jurisdictions in differing time zones enjoying different public holidays, provisions should be inserted in the agreement that if events cannot be dealt with, such as payment of money, on a particular day, they will be dealt with on the next day that banks are open in the relevant country and that notices will only be deemed to be served on days when banks in the country of the recipient would normally be open.

Method of Execution of Formation Agreement

Different methods of execution of agreements apply in each country and advice should be taken as to the proper method of execution. In the case of English companies it should be noted that following the coming into force of the Companies Act 1989, the affixation of the common seal of the company will be optional. In certain circumstances the Formation Agreement may have to be executed in the presence of a notary, or if the document is executed in the presence of a notary certain subsequent filing and registration procedures may be made easier, as may any litigation between the members in certain jurisdictions. While the execution of an agreement before a notary would not be usual in the UK, consideration should be given to such method of execution involving any party in a civil law country.

It is hoped the above will give some guidance as to the nature of the many questions to be considered by prospective founder Members of a Grouping. Although the points covered are particularly relevant to provisions applicable to the formation of any EEIG registered in England and Wales, the same points will have to be considered by and large whichever EC country is chosen for registration of a Grouping.

If the Members, having executed the Formation Agreement, subsequently enter into a separate document or arrangement to regulate in detail the functioning of the Grouping, such later document or arrangement is likely to constitute an amendment to the formation contract and must therefore be filed with the Registrar of Companies and published in the London Gazette and the Official Journal of the Communities.

Language and Format of Formation Agreement

The model contract appearing in Appendix 1 has been drafted in the extended English style and the form of paragraph layout and order of clauses are typical of a contract to which English persons are accustomed. It is quite different from, for example a French or German form of contract. While it may be as time passes that a standardised European format of contract will develop, the format, layout and drafting style of the model may not necessarily be appropriate in other countries of the EC, and equally if may be unacceptable in other EC countries for the contract to be drafted in the English language.

Insofar as a Formation Agreement precedent is used in another language, it is suggested that professional translators be involved to effect the translation and the form of contract be approved by lawyers in the country into whose language the contract has been translated.

Stationery

Prior to the operation of an EEIG, suitable stationery should be prepared and distributed to its Members and managers. The Regulation requires that letters, order forms and similar documents must indicate:

(1) the name of the Grouping preceded or followed by the words 'European Economic Interest Grouping' or the initials 'EEIG', unless those words or initials already occur in the name;
(2) where the Grouping is registered and its number of registration;
(3) the Grouping's official address;
(4) where applicable that the managers must act jointly; and
(5) where applicable that the Grouping is in liquidation.

(6) Competition Law and EEIGs

Application of Competition Law

To date there are no special dispensations for EEIGs from UK or European Competition Law and one must therefore assume that both European and relevant national competition law will apply, as they do to any other undertaking or group of undertakings. There may well be those who consider an EEIG to be a clever device for circumventing competition law on the basis that an EEIG may be exempt from the provisions of EC competition law as its turnover may be minimal and therefore that it will not have an appreciable effect on trade. The structure and objectives of an EEIG, however, are governed by the Formation Agreement between the Members, which for the purposes of competition law constitutes 'an agreement between undertakings'. For this reason, the Competition Law Authorities, including the Office of Fair Trading (OFT) in respect of Competition Law, and the EC Commission ('the Commission') in the case of EC Competition Law, may investigate not only the activities of an EEIG, but also those of its individual Members who are subject to allegations from concerned parties.

Purpose of Competition Law

The basic purpose of competition law is to regulate business to enable free market forces to prevail. Historically, a central feature of the European Community has been to establish a free market in goods and services and to prevent the distortion of trade within the Common Market by anti-competitive practices. An anti-competitive practice would include, for example, an agreement between two business parties, one based in France and the other in West Germany, which might affect trade, whether between those two countries or between either country and another country within the Community. To be anti-competitive, it would not necessarily have to affect trade; it could simply be the intention of the parties for it to do so.

Effects which would infringe competition law include the 'prevention, restriction or distortion of competition'. These are given their broadest possible interpretation and would, for example, include, whether directly or indirectly, the fixing of purchase or selling prices or any other trading conditions.

Business parties entering a Formation Agreement must therefore be very wary of the effects that the EEIG could have on trade. Perhaps the most obvious motive for forming an EEIG would be to combine the resources of businesses operating at the same level in the economy, for example, two manufacturers of spare parts for engines, whether to facilitate research and development, to combine to effect a more efficient marketing operation or to operate as an organ to purchase raw materials for an end product. Clearly, the advantage of forming an EEIG is to enable organisations to combine individual but otherwise complementary businesses under one umbrella.

Nevertheless, these so-called 'horizontal agreements' (the agreements being between parties at the same level of production) have been found to infringe competition law. Businesses considering the formation of an EEIG must therefore obtain specialist legal advice as to any competition aspects of their proposals. Advice will be necessary on a European as well as national level in the countries of the EEIG's official address, its registered office, in the Member's place of operation and wherever it conducts trade.

European Competition Law

Under the Treaty of Rome, agreements between undertakings, decisions by associations of undertakings and concerted practices will be prohibited as incompatible with the Common Market if they:

(1) *may* affect trade between Member States; *and*
(2) have as their object or effect the prevention, restriction or distortion of competition within the Common Market.

There are five instances, in particular, where agreements of this type will be prohibited. These include agreements which:

(a) directly or indirectly fix purchase or selling prices or any other trading conditions;
(b) limit or control production, markets, technical development or investment;
(c) share markets or sources of supply;
(d) apply dissimilar conditions to equivalent transactions with other trading parties, thereby placing them at a competitive disadvantage;
(e) make the conclusion of contracts subject to acceptance by the other party of supplementary obligations which, by their nature or according

to commercial usage, have no connection with the subject of the contracts.

If prohibited, then the agreement or the incompatible provisions will be void and unenforceable. Whether the whole of an agreement is unenforceable will, in practice, depend on the severability of void clauses from the remainder.

Small-Scale Business

The Commission has established guidelines specifying when parties to an agreement will occupy positions in the market deemed too weak for it to have an appreciable effect on trade or competition. An agreement will be deemed to have *no* effect on trade or competition between Member States where:

(1) the goods or services the subject of the agreement represent not more than five per cent of the total market for them; and
(2) the aggregate turnover of the undertakings involved does not exceed ECU200M (approximately £160m).

Both conditions must be satisfied.

Market Share and Turnover

Whereas market share depends on the relevant product and geographic market (in itself posing complex issues) the turnover of the parties includes worldwide turnover net of tax in all goods and services. This includes the turnover of all connected undertakings (which includes all subsidiary and holding and associated companies worldwide) based on the accounts for the last financial year.

The Commission is more likely to investigate the market share and turnover of the underlying Members rather than the EEIG itself. The prudent approach would therefore be for businesses proposing to set up an EEIG to analyse not only the market share and turnover which the EEIG might generate, but also the combined market share and aggregate turnover of each of its Members. For this purpose it is necessary to calculate the turnover of all the holding, subsidiary and associated companies world-wide of each of the Members, and of the EEIG itself.

Although at the time of entering into the Formation Agreement, the guidelines may be complied with, the future growth of the EEIG's business, or that of its Members, must also be considered and a check kept on future developments. If the given levels are exceeded, then (unless exempt, as discussed below) both the Formation Agreement and any agreements between the Members or as between the EEIG and third parties must not contain provisions which would infringe European competition law.

The guideleines are not, however, definitive and do not bind the European Court, which is the court to which EC Competition Law disputes are referred. In the past the Court has held an agreement containing restrictive provisions to be subject to competition law where the market share and turnover of the parties was substantially below the guideline levels referred to above.

Where the turnover or market share of the Members exceeds the given limits (unless exempt, as discussed below) it will be important to avoid including certain types of provision in the Formation Agreement. The same principle applies to agreements between the EEIG and third parties. In the following discussion comments upon the application of European Competition Law to a Formation Agreement apply equally to third party agreements and vice-versa.

Avoiding Infringement of Competition Law

The routes to avoid an infringement of EC Competition Law occurring are briefly described below:

1. *Compliance with the Law*: The competition rules should be complied with in every respect. Where there is any doubt, the parties should first assess their position in the light of available guidelines originating from the Commission. These may prove useful in deciding whether an agreement is valid. They relate to:

(a) Agreements of minor importance (the guidelines on small-scale businesses discussed above).
(b) Co-operation agreements: This guideline deals with certain forms of co-operation agreements where the participators are not actual or potential competitors and there are no adverse effects on third parties.
(c) Exclusive agency contracts: Agreements between a principal and an agent in which the agent agrees, in relation to a specific area of the common market, to procure business or enter agreements on behalf of the principal.
(d) Imports of Japanese products: Arrangements under which it is intended to restrict or control imports of Japanese products into the Community, having as their object or effect the restriction of competition within the Community.
(e) Sub-contracting agreements: Agreements in which a sub-contractor agrees to carry out work in accordance with its contractor's instructions, and for that purpose must utilise certain technology or equipment supplied by the contractor.

Where objectives for setting up an EEIG fall within one of these heads the full text of the guidelines should be considered and appropriate advice should be sought where necessary.

2. *Where the Formation Agreement falls within a 'block exemption'*: The Commission has established various 'block exemptions' to the general competition rules. A block exemption is a device allowing an agreement which may otherwise be void to gain automatic exemption from the rule. It sets out provisions which are allowable (white clauses) and those which are not (black clauses) and other general conditions with which an agreement must comply. Block exemptions have, so far, been granted to cover:

(a) Road and inland waterway transport.
(b) Maritime transport.
(c) Air transport.
(d) Exclusive distribution.
(e) Exclusive purchasing.
(f) Franchising.
(g) Motor vehicle distribution and servicing.
(h) Specialisation.
(i) Research and development.
(j) Patent licensing.
(k) Know-how licensing.

Specific types of agreement falling in the above categories may therefore be able to obtain automatic exemption.

Accordingly, the objectives of the EEIG may enable the Formation Agreement to be structured to obtain the benefit of a block exemption.

3. *Notification of the Formation Agreement to the Commission*: If neither the guidelines nor any block exemption apply, it will be necessary, where there are restrictive conditions of the type detailed above in the Formation Agreement, to notify the Agreement to the Commission. This procedure involves the parties showing that the restrictive conditions will have certain practical benefits. The parties to the Formation Agreement would need to show that the restrictive provisions allow the parties to contribute to the improvement of the production or distribution of goods, or to promoting technical or economical progress. However, three conditions are imposed. The Agreement must:

(a) allow consumers a fair share of the resulting benefit;
(b) not impose on the Members restrictions which are not indispensable to the attainment of those objectives;
(c) not afford the Members the possibility of eliminating competition in respect of a substantial proportion of the products concerned.

Since an EEIG may only be set up for a purpose which is ancillary to its Members, it is probable that an exemption could be successfully obtained by this route. However, notification to the Commission can be a very time-consuming and costly procedure and, except in a few cases, the parties to an agreement should normally seek to use another route.

Examples of Anti-Competitive Agreements Involving EEIGs

One example is where an EEIG is used to carve out a particular product market (supply or purchase). The particular product may only be available from the EEIG. As purchasers of the product would be left without a choice of supplier, this would be likely to affect competition: they would have no alternative but to obtain the product at the price and on the terms and conditions set by the EEIG. An agreement between the members of the EEIG which had such effect would be likely to infringe EC Competition Law.

Restrictions imposed by a Formation Agreement as between the Members which distort competition will be void. Restrictions which might distort competition could include the application of dissimilar conditions to each of the Members, or the imposition of minimum purchase or annual turnover obligations upon them. For example, if an EEIG is formed to purchase spare parts for aircraft for a common pool then if the Members are obliged to purchase minimum quantities of spare parts from the pool or to maintain a certain annual turnover of spares taken from it, this could distort competition if, as a result, the Members were in practice unable to purchase spare parts elsewhere.

Anti-competitive restrictions of a subjective nature in a Formation Agreement are likely to be void, as would be the case with restrictions adopted to prevent Members from promoting, marketing or selling any product or item of equipment which in the opinion of the other Members is *competitive or potentially competitive* with any of the products dealt in. Such products are likely to be products dealt in by each of its Members since an EEIG's business will be ancillary to that of its Members. Where a restriction of this type is required, an EEIG should consider confining it to promoting, marketing or selling any product or item of equipment which is of the *same kind or description* as the products dealt in by the EEIG.

If the Members of an EEIG seek an exemption from the Commission to the general rule that an agreement containing restrictions of the prohibited kind are void, the Commission will assess whether the restrictions in the agreement are indispensable to the attainment of the EEIG's objectives. An exemption will only be given if, in the Commission's view, the derived benefits will not be attainable with any less restriction than the restrictive practice would entail.

The point can be illustrated by an example of four companies which form an EEIG to facilitate their production and distribution of a particular type of microchip, where a restriction on each individual Member preventing it from producing and marketing the microchip alone, is a pre-requisite of reaching the EEIG's objective. If at the outset each Member is able to produce and market the microchip on his own, the restriction would fail the test and the exemption would not be granted. However, if it is only possible for the chip to be made with the combined resources of the four companies together, the test should be passed. For one of them subsequently to produce and market the microchip on its own would deprive the EEIG of a goal which at the outset no one Member could have achieved. In other words, the goal could only be achieved by combining its resources and talents with those of the other Members. A restriction on each of the parties to prevent them promoting, marketing or selling a microchip of the same kind or description would not seem to be unreasonable and might well obtain the benefit of an exemption from the Commission.

Penalties for Breach of EC Competition Law

For non-compliance with European competition law, the Commission has the power to impose fines on undertakings or associations of undertakings. Fines could therefore be imposed upon an EEIG or its individual Members. The fines are severe. They range from ECUs 1,000 to ECUs 1,000,000 (approximately £600 to £600,000). A fine of a greater sum not exceeding 10 per cent of the turnover in the preceding business year of each of the undertakings participating in the infringement could be charged.

It is unclear whether the 10 per cent rule will relate to the turnover of the EEIG or also include the turnover of its Members. Nevertheless, if the Formation Agreement, any subsequent agreement between the Members, or any agreement between the EEIG and a third party, infringes the competition rules discussed above, substantial fines could therefore be levied. Individual Members would have joint and several liability.

UK Competition Law

The two major provisions of UK Competition Law relevant to EEIGs are the Competition Act 1980 and the Restrictive Trade Practices Act 1976, although this latter Act is likely to be repealed and replaced by new laws set out in a UK government 'white paper'.

Competition Act 1980

This Act gives power to the Director General of Fair Trading at the OFT to investigate and refer to the Monopolies and Mergers Commission 'anti-competitive practices' between two parties in the UK. It provides for an 'anti-competitive practice' procedure. This permits the investigation of anti-competitive practices and procedures of organisations and of agreements imposed by them. In practice, the OFT operates on complaints from the public or traders.

The Act will not apply where a concerned party, including any other Members of its group, has a turnover of less than £5m and the products covered by the anti-competitive practice represent less than five per cent of the relevant market. This rule is operated in a similar way to the Commission guidelines on minor agreements. The OFT could consider not only the turnover and market share of the EEIG, but also that of each of its Members. Therefore similar considerations to those already discussed apply.

Restrictive Trade Practices Act 1976 (RTPA)

The RTPA 1976 applies to any agreement between two or more parties who carry on business in the UK, given certain conditions. The parties will be involved in the production or supply of goods or in the application of any process of manufacture to them. But two or more parties (not necessarily those based in the UK) will have accepted trading restrictions. Examples of the restrictions covered include:

(a) any restrictions on prices (even those to be recommended or suggested as prices to be quoted in resale);
(b) terms and conditions of supply or purchase;
(c) terms and conditions as to the persons or classes of person to, for, or from whom goods are to be supplied or acquired;
(d) terms and conditions as to the areas in or from which goods are to be supplied or acquired.

Except in very limited circumstances, this type of agreement must be registered in the Official Register of Registrable Agreements maintained by the OFT. Registration must be made either before the agreement takes effect or within three months after the date of the agreement whichever is earlier.

Members and managers of an EEIG must therefore assess the Formation Agreement and terms of any agreements entered into by the EEIG. Failure to register a registerable agreement within the prescribed time limit will mean that the relevant restrictions are void. It is unlawful to give effect to void restrictions. Therefore, any third party suffering a loss as a result will be able to bring an action in damages against the EEIG for breach of its statutory duty. As stated, the liability of Members is joint and several; consequently it is the Members themselves who would incur responsibility for payment of damages.

The 1989 Proposals to Replace the RTPA 1976

The RTPA 1976 is due to be replaced. This may happen in 1990 or 1991. The proposed new Act will adopt an economic analysis of trading arrangements (and their effects on trade) in place of the highly automatic approach of the RTPA. It is intended to replace the RTPA with legislation having a similar effect to European competition law. For example, where an agreement has the benefit of an EC block exemption, it will also be exempt under the new legislation.

The proposals are contained in the recent Government White Paper entitled 'Opening Markets: New Policy on Restrictive Trade Practices'. Many agreements not caught by the RTPA will, if the paper is adopted, be caught by its replacement.

The penalties for infringement will be severe. Business directors and managers will be individually liable to fines of up to £100,000 if responsible for having negotiated or put into effect an infringing agreement. This is sure to have more impact than simply imposing fines on the undertaking concerned.

The implications for an EEIG are not fully known. However, either those responsible for its management and administration, or its Members and those whose individual responsibility it was for the EEIG entering into an infringing agreement, may be liable.

As proposed, the new Act will (subject to a one year transitional period) be retrospective. It would therefore be prudent to structure arrangements to comply with European competition law at the outset, not later. As mentioned, the approach is similar to European Competition Law. If complied with, arrangements will be less likely to infringe the new Act. Otherwise, once adopted, it may become necessary to re-negotiate terms and re-draft contracts, in which case both management and legal costs would be wasted. Furthermore, any third party who has suffered loss as a result of an infringing agreement will be able to claim damages or injunctions against the businesses which have failed to comply. Action could be taken against the EEIG or its Members. It is important to recognise the scope this provision would have. The UK Government intends that it will have a similar effect to US anti-trust legislation. Private actions should become an important mechanism for enforcement of competition law. The practice may, nevertheless, be different to the theory.

The Government is determined to secure a free market. Responsibility for enforcing the new legislation will lie with the OFT and a new body, the Restrictive Practices Tribunal. New powers will be created. The OFT will be allowed to enter business premises, with the use of force if necessary, to investigate breaches or suspected breaches of the Act. Under European competition law Commission officials have similar powers. Historically, they have been an extremely powerful weapon for enforcing competition law. Inspectors would be entitled to examine agreements, letters or other records, and to take copies of them. It is therefore important that each Member as well as the EEIG administrators ensure compliance at all times.

At the outset and throughout its life, the practice and procedure of the EEIG will need to be kept under review. This includes the policies of the EEIG and agreements between the Members or the EEIG and third parties. The threat of investigation, and possibility of substantial fines against the Managers (or administrators), will make this review essential.

Appropriate Legal Advice

The formation and running of an EEIG is likely to have consequences under local (eg UK) and European competition law. Local consequences may occur in the country of the EEIG's official address, registered office or place of operation and wherever it conducts trade.

Throughout its life specialist legal advice will therefore be required to ensure an EEIG and its Members comply with European and local competition law.

(7) What are the Registration Procedures for a Grouping in EC Member States?

Initial Registration in the State where the Offical Address is Situated

In essence, the procedure for formation of a Grouping is straightforward. The Members must execute their Formation Agreement setting out the minimum requirements of the Regulation and such other requirements as the Members may agree; send the same to the appropriate Registry in the relevant country; pay a fee and advertise the creation of the Grouping in one or more official journals.

Further Registrations

If a Grouping establishes itself in a Member State other than that in which it has its official address, it must also be registered in that Member State. Such registration is achieved by sending copies of those documents required for registration of the Grouping to the Registry of its official address. Any further documents required by the Regulation to be sent to the Registry in the country in which the Grouping has its official address must also be sent to the Registry in the Member State in which the Grouping has its establishment. The rationale for this requirement is that it gives protection to creditors and other third parties dealing with the Grouping, by providing information about the Grouping.

Since, for the purposes of registering EEIGs, Scotland, England and Wales and Northern Ireland are separate jurisdictions, a Grouping established in, eg Northern Ireland and England and Wales will need to be registered in Belfast and Cardiff. Equally a Grouping established in both England and Scotland will need to be registered in Edinburgh, as well as Cardiff.

As stated earlier, the registration procedures for EEIGs vary from one Member State to another. These are summarised in Appendix II.

Check-list of Points to Consider When Forming an EEIG

This check-list is only a guide to matters which may need to be considered when forming each EEIG and expert advice should be taken in each case on the specific facts.

CHAPTER FOUR
TAXATION AND ACCOUNTING ISSUES

The creation of a new business form is always a challenge and an opportunity for those involved in giving advice on taxation and accounting issues. In the UK, although there have been significant developments at the margins, there have been no substantial changes in the legal entities through which business can be done for many years. Most of the major developments took place in the nineteenth century. It is not, therefore, surprising that for those within the profession and for many outside, the passing of Council Regulation (EEC 1985/2137) and its coming into force on 1 July 1989 have generated considerable interest. That interest has been heightened by the fact that the Grouping is, by definition, an international entity which must necessarily involve the interaction of the tax, legal and accounting systems of more than one Member State.

The aim of this chapter is to explore primarily the taxation framework for Groupings, as it has been determined at the level of the European Commission and in the Member States themselves. The main focus will be on the recent UK tax legislation, introduced in the Finance Act 1990, but the Grouping is a cross-border concept and the UK position cannot be looked at in isolation. There will, therefore, be comments on the developing tax legislation in other Member States.

Before addressing the taxation aspects however, there are a number of points to be made on the accounting framework for groupings, particularly as it relates to UK registered Groupings and participation in them by UK companies.

Accounting Issues

In the UK, the accounting issues for Groupings themselves have, to a large extent, been simplified. There is no requirement for a Grouping to produce accounts for Companies Act purposes. The United Kingdom European Economic Interest Grouping Regulations (1989/638) does not incorporate any of the Companies Act provisions in this area and the Regulation itself is equally silent on the obligation to prepare and publish accounts for a Grouping. In most cases, it seems likely that the Members of a UK registered Grouping will want the Grouping's accounts to be audited, in order to protect their interests. This is normal practice for joint ventures. However, the format and disclosure will, in the absence of any specific requirements, be a matter for the Members to determine, although they will have to be sufficiently detailed to enable Inland Revenue to calculate any tax liability which may arise from the Grouping's activities.

The legal position is not the same in other EC countries. Several Member States will impose a requirement to produce audited accounts, but, typically, this will affect the larger groupings where, by reason of turnover or number of employees, they reach the domestic threshold for companies to have accounts audited or available for public inspection.

In the UK the accounting issue which is most likely to give rise to debate will be the impact of Exposure Draft 49 and the Companies Act 1989 on the requirements for consolidation of a UK company's interest in a Grouping. In broad terms, Exposure Draft 49 represents the latest thoughts of the Accounting Standards Committee on 'Accounting for special purpose transactions' which has, as its focus, the circumstances in which 'off balance sheet' treatment may be adopted in the UK. The Companies Act 1989 essentially enacted the Seventh Company Law Directive. This is not the place for a detailed discussion of 'off balance sheet' accounting. However, a number of brief comments can be made in the context of Groupings.

There is no requirement for a Grouping to have capital of any type and, indeed, there is no provision in the Regulation for a Grouping to have capital divided into shares. There is, therefore, no question of a company holding a majority of the shares in a Grouping and, for that reason, being required to produce consolidated accounts, but, under the provisions of the Companies Act 1989, this is only one of a number of tests that have to be applied in determining whether the results of the Grouping should be consolidated with its Members. Of these, the ability to exercise voting control or a 'dominant influence' are considered significant.

Under Art 17 of the Regulation, it is expressly provided that no one Member should hold a majority of the votes in a Grouping and many of the major decisions affecting a Grouping require a unanimous decision by the Members. In this context, it is difficult to see that a normal Grouping will give control of votes, control of the Board, or control of policy to any one Member. A situation where one UK company participates in a Grouping through its UK and French subsidiaries will, of course, be a different matter, but where the Members are independent, these control tests would seem not to be met.

There will clearly be some situations in which an individual member of a Grouping has a dominant influence over it. This could apply for example where one Member held 50 per cent of the votes and the remaining 50 per cent was fragmented through 10 other Members. However, this situation may be rare. It would not be difficult to imagine a Grouping with three Members, eg a UK company, a German company and a French company, who each had equal rights over profits and assets and who shared voting rights equally. In that situation, there might be a strong argument that the UK Member would not have to consolidate the results of the Grouping, but merely bring them in through the equity accounting method. The position in the other jurisdictions might, however, be different.

In some respects, the situation could be likened to that of participation in a 'normal' consortium company, but there may be other advantages, including tax advantages, in operating through a Grouping, which would make this form more attractive.

Even where agreement can be reached that a particular interest in a Grouping should be off balance sheet, there seems certain to be some debate between industry and the profession over the extent of any disclosure of the participation in the Grouping in the notes to the accounts of the Member. The provisions of Art 24 of the Regulation which impose unlimited joint and several liability on the Members of the Grouping 'for its debts and other liabilities' supports the case for some more detailed disclosure of the participation in the notes to the accounts of a UK Member. However, these are very judgmental areas which would need to be addressed on a case by case basis.

If the accounting issues can be dealt with very briefly, that is certainly not the case for the taxation issues. The position is complex at both the level of the Member and of the Grouping itself and in order to understand the complexities fully, it is necessary to consider the interaction of the European Commission's intent and its implementation in the Member States.

Taxation: the Commission's Approach

General

It is not difficult to find evidence of the Commission's intent in creating the Grouping. In the official publication of the Commission on this subject[1] it is stated quite simply:

> 'EEIGs are intended to facilitate transnational co-operation .... The objective of the new instrument is to encourage co-operation among companies based in several Member States of the Community.'

This important statement establishes the Commission's rationale for creating this new business entity and gives rise to the general expectation that in determining the legal framework, the taxation system and the operational management of these entities, the Commission will have followed that broad general intent.

[1]'European File, The European Economic Interest Grouping (EEIG), A new instrument for economic co-operation in the community' April 1989, at p 3.

The Recitals to the Regulation echo this theme. The text reads:

> 'It is necessary that ... natural persons, companies, firms and other legal bodies should be able to co-operate effectively across frontiers.'

It recognises that ... 'co-operation of this nature can encounter legal, fiscal or psychological difficulties' and declares that this new business entity will contribute to the achievement of the objective of effective cross-border co-operation.

The extent to which the Commission has achieved its objective in other spheres has been considered in earlier chapters. There has certainly been an attempt to create a flexible legal regime which permits many of the benefits of a corporate structure to be achieved without the complexities which normally attend them in most jurisdictions. This simplicity and flexibility will, no doubt, appeal to many companies and individuals and would, therefore, tend to encourage the use of Groupings. In the taxation field, it would have been logical to expect to see that mirrored by the introduction of a tax regime which would simplify some of the complexities inherent in cross-border ventures.

Taxation Framework

The solution adopted by the Commission in setting the taxation framework for Groupings appears indeed to be simplicity itself. Article 40 of the Regulation simply states:

> 'The profits or losses resulting from the activities of a Grouping shall be taxable only in the hands of its Members.'

and the Recitals supplement this with the words:

> 'It is understood that otherwise national tax laws apply, particularly as regards the apportionment of profits, tax procedures and any obligations imposed by national tax law.'

It would have been difficult to ask for a more concise statement of the Commission's intent: Art 40 provides the framework of fiscal transparency and the Recitals simply tidy up the peripheral areas. The Regulation avoids the pitfall of tax jargon and Art 40 sounds as if it should be capable of interpretation by the layman as easily as by the tax lawyer. Even in the way in which it puts responsibility for taxation in the hands of the Grouping's Members, it suggests that tax is simply not an issue for a Grouping. However, in doing so it lays a trap for the unwary. A number of commentators have been misled into suggesting that because the wording of Art 40 is clear and simple, the taxation consequences that flow from it must be equally simple. Unfortunately, this is far from the truth. Article 40 has been very carefully drafted. It means precisely what it says - and no more - and its interpretation is a matter of fine detail.

Article 40: Interpretation

The first and most obvious point of Art 40 is that it does not permit the Member States to tax the Grouping itself on its profits. It treats the Members of the Grouping as having earned those profits and permits tax to be levied in respect of them only on those Members. In effect, it treats the Grouping as an international partnership with tax attributes passing through directly to the Members or partners.

It is important, however, to recognise that in arriving at this analysis, the Commission has had to make two fundamental decisions: first that a Grouping can make profits (or losses); and secondly, that a Grouping should only be fiscally transparent to the extent of tax on those profits (or losses). It should not be transparent for other tax purposes. Both of these points merit closer examination.

Profits and losses

The opening words of Art 40 are: 'The profits or losses resulting from the activities of a Grouping . . .' On a first reading, these words seem to be in direct conflict with the basic concept of a Grouping, namely that it should exist only to support the activities of its Members through some ancillary function. However, this is not the case. Although Art 3 says that 'The purpose of a Grouping . . . is not to make profits for itself'. . ., nevertheless, the Commission has recognised that a Grouping can make profits, whether or not that is its principal purpose and that, as a result, a proper framework for the taxation of those profits should be put in place.

There has been a great deal of debate about this issue, particularly among commentators in the Member States themselves. It has been argued that if a Grouping is not permitted to make profits for itself, it cannot have a business purpose and concepts of business taxation should not, therefore, apply. This has been a particularly contentious issue in Germany, where the distinction is of some importance.

As a result of this debate, it has been broadly acknowledged that there may be two types of Groupings, one type which is engaged in activities purely of a support nature and another type which does engage in a normal business activity. It is to this latter category that the provisions of Art 40 are particularly directed.

Application

The second point is that the adoption of Art 40 in its present form imposed strict limits on the application of fiscal transparency. Article 40 requires that the profits or losses resulting from the activities of the Grouping should be taxable in the hands of its Members but it is entirely silent on the application of taxation in its other forms.

The Recitals provide the answer to this silence in the words 'otherwise national tax laws apply'. This statement needs to be read very widely. It was not the Commission's intention that the principle of fiscal transparency set out in Art 40 should apply to any other aspect of taxation than the treatment of profits or losses arising from its activities. Consequently, as far as the Regulation is concerned the Grouping is responsible, like any other business, for the collection, administration and payment of other taxes, for example, employee payroll taxes and social security, VAT, transfer duties on the acquisition or disposal of assets and customs duties. Where local taxes are levied other than on a profit-related basis, those taxes will continue to be levied on the Grouping.

In a similar way, transactions, other than those which give rise to profits or losses in the Grouping, will fall under the normal rules of the Member State concerned. There is no special regime, even for transactions between a Grouping and its Members.

The result of the Commission's deliberations is, therefore, a hybrid entity which does not fit comfortably into the structure of either corporate or individual taxation. It cannot stand alone for tax purposes and yet the economic unity of the Grouping with its Members is incomplete. In many countries, it puts a Grouping, and the Members' relationship with it, into one of the most difficult and complex areas of domestic tax law. In the international context, it makes a Grouping a vehicle which needs to be approached with some care.

Article 40: International Tax Implications

Before looking at the way in which the individual Member States have carried through the Commission's taxation objectives into their domestic legislation, it is important to understand how the basic concept of the Grouping, as set out in the Regulation, fits into the general scheme of international taxation. The Grouping is unique in its availability as a business entity in the same form in a number of different countries, in its ability to move its registered office between them and, to some extent, in its hybrid characteristics. These features give rise to some tax issues in the international context which are rarely met elsewhere.

The main international issues which a rise from the Commission's approach are in the areas of tax residence, the application of the permanent establishment concept, the taxation of capital gains and asset contributions. The most complex of these is residence.

Residence

The Grouping has been conceived of as an international entity. Under the terms of the Regulation, it must have Members from at least two countries in the EC.

It will, therefore, inevitably be involved in cross-border transactions and the issue of the fiscal residence of the Grouping will need to be considered to determine taxing rights and the availability of relief.

The residence status of the entity for domestic purposes is a matter for the internal law of the Member States and will be considered at a later point. However, residence for international tax purposes is a matter for treaty law and the result of the application of treaty law follows on logically from the framework imposed by the Commission. Broadly, it is likely that a Grouping will not be resident for tax treaty purposes either in the jurisdiction of its formation or in a jurisdiction in which it carries out its business activities. Indeed, it will not have a fiscal residence at all except in some very specific situations.

The reason for this is the interaction between the tax treatment of the Grouping under Art 40 and the theory of residence adopted in Art 4 of the OECD Model Treaty. Art 4 states:

> 'For the purposes of this Convention, the term "resident of a Contracting State" means any person who, under the laws of that State, is liable to tax therein by reason of his domicile, residence, place of management or any other criterion of a similar nature. But this term does not include any person who is liable to tax in that State in respect only of income from sources in that State or capital situated therein.'

Since the profits of a Grouping are taxable only in the hands of its Members, it is not 'liable to tax' at all and will, therefore, fail the basic test of Art 4 even where, under the internal law of a particular jurisdiction, a Grouping is considered resident for domestic tax purposes.

The implications of this are seen most clearly in the application of the OECD Model Treaty Articles on interest and royalties in the context of a Grouping. Where a Grouping pays interest or royalties cross-border, there will normally be an issue as to whether the payments can be made free from withholding tax and, if so, on what authority. Some jurisdictions impose no withholding tax under domestic law, but in many countries, interest and royalties paid to non-residents will be subject to withholding tax unless exempted by an applicable tax treaty.

The Model Treaty provides for interest arising in a Contracting State to be taxed in the State of the recipient but allows the State of source to impose a maximum tax charge of 10 per cent of the gross interest. In the case of royalties, the taxing rights are given exclusively to the recipient. The first point to note is that the application of the interest or royalty article is not dependent on the *payer* being a resident of a Contracting State. It only requires that the *recipient* be a resident of one of the States and the *source* of the payment be in the other. Recipients of interest and royalty payments from a Grouping will, therefore, enjoy the benefits available under the relevant treaty between the State of source and the recipient's State of residence, irrespective of the fact that the Grouping itself may have no residence.

The second point to note, however, under Art 11(5) of the Model Treaty, is that where a person who may, or may not, be a resident of one of the Contracting States has a permanent establishment in one of the States and the interest (this provision applies only to interest) is borne by the permanent establishment, that interest can be deemed to arise in the State in which the permanent establishment exists. In certain circumstances, this could mean that a withholding might apply where interest was paid by a Grouping which might not apply if it was paid direct by the Member or Members concerned. This is difficult to follow in isolation and an example may, therefore, help to clarify the point.

Take a UK registered Grouping with a UK and French corporate Member. The Grouping pays interest to Spain. There is no withholding requirement on a French company paying interest abroad, but the UK/France Treaty regards the interest borne by any permanent establishment in the UK as UK source interest. So too does the UK/Spain Treaty. The UK imposes a requirement to deduct tax at a rate of 25 per cent on interest paid to a non-resident which, under the treaty with Spain, is reduced to 12 per cent. It would, therefore, appear that the UK Revenue Authorities could require a withholding of 12 per cent to be operated on interest payments made by the Grouping to the Spanish recipient (assuming that the Grouping was carrying on a trade in the UK) whereas the French Member could have paid interest to Spain direct, free from withholding. Not every situation will be as complex or as difficult as this, but it highlights the need to address the interaction of domestic and treaty law in considering the viability of particular financing arrangements for a Grouping.

The position is again complex where the Grouping is the recipient of interest or royalty payments. Here, the result may, potentially, be even less satisfactory than where the Grouping is the payer.

Under the normal application of commercial law, the Grouping will have the full ability to contract with third parties. It may, therefore, choose either to lend money to residents of other States, or to license intangible property rights in return for a royalty. From the point of view of the payer, he will be making payments to the Grouping and not to its Members. He may not even be aware who the Members are. However, while the Members might have been entitled to a reduced rate of withholding under a treaty between their State of residence and that of the payer, no such benefit may accrue to the Grouping. The rationale for this is that the Grouping has no residence under most treaties and cannot, therefore, claim the benefit of the reduced withholding if the particular treaty in point is in Model Treaty form. To the extent that the authorities in the State of the payer require certification of the residence or taxpaying status of the Grouping from the authorities in its State of registration, a request for treaty relief in relation to the Grouping may be rejected.

The alternative method of seeking treaty relief would be to make the application in the name of the Members rather than in that of the Grouping. However, the authorities in the payer's jurisdiction may again reject such a claim on the basis that the legal arrangements are with the Grouping, which has full capacity to contract, and not with the Members and, therefore, such an application would not be in point. Even if those authorities were to accept that the Members could make a valid claim, given the nature of the Grouping, each Member would need to make a separate application under the treaty between its own jurisdiction and that of the payer. Unless all the treaties gave a nil rate of withholding or a consistent rate of withholding was applied, the result could be that a variety of withholdings would have to be made from each royalty or interest payment, reflecting the treaty relationship with the individual Members and the proportionate interest of each of the Members in the interest or royalty stream. This would give rise to very complex results and would, potentially, make the administration of some Groupings very unwieldy.

A further complication is the absence of a full treaty network between the Members of the EC. Greece and Portugal, for instance, have treaties with a relatively small number of countries. Not every Grouping will, therefore, be able to claim treaty relief, even for its dealings within the EC, a situation which will add to the uncertainty surrounding the treatment of Groupings.

It is understood that approaches have been made by individual Revenue Authorities within the European community to their counterparts in certain non-EC countries, with a view to establishing how the Groupings will be treated by those countries. However, at the time of writing, that position has yet to be clarified.

Permanent establishment

The second major issue in the international context, and one which follows on naturally from the question of residence, is whether a Grouping will constitute a permanent establishment of its Members in either the country of its registration or (if it is different) in the countries in which it operates and whether the Members will be considered to be carrying on a business through it. This will normally determine whether its activities will be regarded as constituting a taxable presence there. A Member's share of the Grouping's business profits will be liable to tax in a particular State to the extent that they are attributable to a permanent establishment in that State.

Single country operations

The OECD Model Treaty defines a 'permanent establishment' as 'a fixed place of business through which the business of an enterprise is wholly or partly carried on' (Art 5(1)). The model wording provides a number of examples of a permanent establishment and also some guidance on activities which would fall outside the definition. Among them is an exclusion for 'the maintenance of a fixed place of business solely for the purpose of carrying on, for the enterprise, any . . . activity of a preparatory or auxiliary character' (Art 5(4)(e)). It is these tests which are primarily at issue here. Where the Grouping has a business presence in a Member State and neither this nor another exclusion applies, the Members of the Grouping will normally be subject to tax in that jurisdiction on their share of the results of the activities attributable to that presence. However, where an exclusion from permanent establishment status does apply or where as a matter of fact, the Grouping does not carry on business through a permanent establishment in a particular State, the Members may be regarded as having no taxable presence in that jurisdiction by virtue of the Grouping.

There has been considerable debate in the Member States as to how the 'permanent establishment' Article should be applied in the context of a Grouping. Some commentators have cast doubt on whether a Member can actually carry on all or part of his business through a Grouping given the constraints in the Regulation and argued that the basic test in Art 5(1) cannot, therefore, be met.

Others have suggested that, because a Grouping is required under the Regulation not to engage in any activities that are more than 'ancillary' to those of its Members, it must automatically be within the exclusion provided in Art 5(4)(e) of the Model Treaty for activities of an 'auxiliary' character.

However, it is clear from statements made by the Commission that it is their intention that the 'ancillary' test in Art 3 of the Regulation should be interpreted very widely. They see no barrier to the idea of Groupings carrying on normal business activities (albeit with a view to benefiting their members rather than the Groupings themselves) and envisage that a business carried on by a Grouping could encompass almost anything short of the entire activities of the Member.

This is something which may ultimately have to be tested before the European Court of Justice. Some commentators have already taken a narrower view of what the Regulation actually says and this may ultimately be more important than the expressed intention of the Commission. However, if the wider view can be relied upon, it will create the clear possibility of Groupings which fail the auxiliary test in Art 5 of the Model Treaty. Certainly, if a Grouping is carrying on an active business, it would seem likely to be treated under Art 5 as a permanent establishment of its Members. Most Revenue Authorities interpret this Article somewhat narrowly, in line with the guidance given in the Commentary to the OECD Model Treaty.

There is one further point which makes it more likely that a Grouping will be treated as constituting a permanent establishment. Most Revenue Authorities apply the principle that if an entity such as a representative office supplies services to more than one 'enterprise' – even to two members of the same affiliated Group – it falls outside the exclusions provided by Art 5(4) because it services more than 'the enterprise'. A Grouping, by definition, must always exist to serve at least two Members. Arguably, it will, therefore, always fail the auxiliary/preparatory activities test. This would be an exceptionally harsh interpretation of the Treaty provisions but there is evidence to suggest that at least some of the Revenue Authorities may deem all Groupings, including those entirely remote from a profit function, permanent establishments because of this feature inherent in their legal form.

Third country operations

Although many Groupings will operate only within the boundaries of the country in which they are registered and will, therefore, fall within that tax regime and ultimately the tax regime of their Members, it is likely that many will also have operations in one or more other jurisdictions. In these cases, the issue will be essentially whether the third country operations would enjoy any treaty protection and if so which treaty would apply.

The starting point is Art 7 of the OECD Model Treaty which states that:

> 'The profits of an enterprise of a Contracting State shall be taxable only in that State, unless the enterprise carries on business in the other Contracting State through a permanent establishment situated therein'

These are familiar words to those involved in international tax work, as indeed are the complementary words of Art 5, referred to above, which define the term 'permanent establishment', for treaty purposes, as 'a fixed place of business through which the business of an enterprise is wholly or partly carried on'. The phrase 'enterprise of a Contracting State' is defined in Art 3 as 'an enterprise carried on by a resident of a Contracting State'.

We have already seen that, under OECD concepts, a Grouping is not resident in any jurisdiction for treaty purposes. From that analysis, it follows that neither Art 7 nor Art 5, to the extent that they rely on the underlying principle of residence, can apply and the benefits of Art 7, limiting the rights of the local jurisdiction to impose tax, cannot accrue to the Grouping itself.[2]

The issue is, therefore, whether the Grouping is denied treaty protection altogether or whether the permanent establishment test can be applied in the context of the relationship between the Members of the Grouping and the overseas business activity. If so, it would presumably need to be applied separately under the treaties of each of the individual Members.

Looking through the Grouping in this way, to its Members, would in most cases be more attractive than leaving the operations without treaty protection. However, the basis for doing so seems uncertain. In an EC context, it is possible, perhaps likely, that the Authorities would take that approach, following the reasoning that the overseas operations are no more and no less than a business carried on by an EC resident albeit two steps removed. In a non-EC context this result seems less likely, given the legal personality of the Grouping and given the normally narrow interpretation of the definition of 'enterprise' for the purposes of Art 5(4) of the Model Treaty.

[2]There is an argument that the term 'business of an enterprise' in Art 5(1) can be interpreted more generously where it lacks the qualification 'of a Contracting State' so as to bring Groupings within its scope, but this may be open to doubt.

Whether they enjoy any treaty protection or not, it seems very likely that there will be many Groupings whose profits fall to be taxed in a jurisdiction other than that of their registration. Those whose activities are more than merely preparatory or auxiliary will almost certainly fall into that category in third countries.

The position may become highly complex, particularly where Groupings have business activities in non-EC countries. Even within the EC, there are likely to be complexities in determining the appropriate allocation of profits and tax to the Grouping's Members. Given the existence of both the credit and exemption methods of dealing with permanent establishments within the EC, there is a strong possibility that the combined level of taxation suffered as a result of doing business through a Grouping will differ quite substantially from the result of that same activity being carried out by a single company. This may well be an area which proves to be a breeding ground for competent authority claims, but given the generally slow and cumbersome nature of that process, and the discretionary element within it, this may not be a satisfactory method of resolving the disputes that arise.

Other issues

Two other points need to be aired in the context of the permanent establishment issue although the answers may not be clarified in the various jurisdictions for some time. Both relate to the funding of the Grouping.

Although the Regulation does not require a Grouping to have capital of any sort and indeed makes no provision for it, it seems likely that in some cases the Revenue Authorities will seek to deny Members of a Grouping a full deduction for the Grouping's interest costs if it is funded entirely with debt. It would be surprising if they did not insist upon at least a measure of free capital or deemed free capital. This may become an issue not only for the Grouping itself, but also for any permanent establishment it might have in a third country.

It is possible that there will also be some difficulties over the deductibility of interest paid on any loans from Members to a Grouping. This may, again, be a complex issue, particularly where a deduction for interest borne by a permanent establishment is specifically permitted under certain treaties but not under others. It is possible, therefore, to envisage a situation where a Grouping or its permanent establishment will be able to obtain a deduction for only part of its interest expense.

Capital gains

There is currently great divergence, internationally, in the direct taxation of capital gains. Exemptions exist within jurisdictions for particular types of assets, which are not matched in other jurisdictions. Certain transactions qualify for relief in some Member States but not in others and the time at which gains are crystallised may differ. Some countries have significantly reduced rates of tax for long term gains while others have provisions which defer tax arising on certain business assets where reinvestment is made in qualifying categories of assets. In the context of a Grouping, there seems a particular risk that these differences will give rise to many anomalous taxation consequences. In particular, there must be a concern that the Grouping may be unable to carry out some transactions which might benefit the majority of Members, because of an adverse taxation result caused by the interaction of the different tax systems involved.

Asset contributions

The fourth major international tax issue is the taxation of the transfer of property – particularly appreciated property – into or out of the Grouping.

In the context of a joint venture, it is common for companies or individuals to contribute assets to the joint venture vehicle. The transfers may be of plant and equipment or other tangible or intangible property. In the case of a transfer to a Grouping, it seems likely that this could trigger an immediate tax cost, potentially in three forms: a transfer tax, a recapture of tax depreciation and a capital gains tax.

If the property transferred is subject to transfer taxes, these would apply on a transfer into a Grouping. While in the UK, a maximum stamp duty cost of one per cent might not represent a major burden, the position could be very different, say, in France with a tax in excess of 14 per cent on some property transfers. On some categories of assets, the transferor could suffer a recapture of tax depreciation previously granted; and if appreciated property was transferred into the Grouping it seems likely that most Authorities would treat the transfer as at least a partial disposal and tax the transferring Member as if it had realised a gain. In some jurisdictions, the gain may not be crystallised if the transfer is into a locally registered Grouping. However, to the extent that a tax charge does apply on the transfer of property into a Grouping, it seems likely to act as a significant deterrent to companies or individuals considering doing business through a Grouping since it imposes a real cost on the setting up process, at a point at which there may be no obvious or immediate compensation.

Taken together, the four generic issues discussed above could constitute a significant obstacle for individuals or companies thinking of setting up and using a Grouping. They are certainly points which will need careful attention in the planning stage. A single example may provide a useful summary.

Take the example of a Grouping, set up to engage in research and development work but carrying out sufficient activities to be regarded as trading.

(1) On the setting up of the Grouping, there may be a tax charge on a Member transferring appreciated property into the Grouping.

(2) Interest borne by the Grouping may be only partially deductible for tax purposes either because of a 'free capital' issue or because of the absence of a suitable provision in a relevant treaty specifically permitting deductibility.
(3) Interest paid cross-border may be subject to a variety of rates of withholding, depending on the applicable treaties of the Members.
(4) Disparities in the taxation systems of Members of the Grouping may result in more than 100 per cent of the profits of the Grouping being subject to tax.
(5) If the research and development programme gives rise to royalties payable to the Grouping, those payments may be subject to rates of withholding tax dictated by the relevant treaties of the Members rather than the Grouping itself; or alternatively, there may be no treaty relief since the Members are not the legal recipients of the payments.
(6) On the breaking up of a Grouping, there may be further capital gains charges if property has appreciated during ownership by the Grouping, even if the property ultimately reverts to its original owner.

This does not immediately sound like a tax regime to encourage cross-border co-operation!

The Commission's Approach: Summary

There is some difficulty in rationalising the logic of the Commission in, on the one hand, encouraging companies and individuals to co-operate on a cross-border basis, while, on the other, not providing a taxation framework which also encourages co-operation or at least makes the position neutral. Commercial logic suggests that if the aim is indeed to encourage cross-border co-operation between separate entities so as to 'stimulate transnational economic co-operation, economic growth and the integration of the economies of Community Member countries', the way to achieve that, through the taxation system, would be to allow a Member of a Grouping to be subject to no additional taxes as a result of co-operating with another EC business than if he had carried out those activities on his own. This approach could have encompassed, in particular, forms of hold-over relief or tax deferral on the transfer of assets to a Grouping on its formation, and on their extraction on a dissolution or on the incorporation of a Grouping into a more traditional corporate form in one of the Member States.

However, the Commission has taken as its brief, the creation of a taxation framework in which the Members of a Grouping will be taxed, not on the same basis as if they had carried out their activities alone, but on a basis as close as possible to the taxation treatment of business entities which already co-operate through other legal forms. They have been particularly concerned to ensure that the use of Groupings should offer no tax advantages. To this extent they can justifiably claim to have created a level playing field, but from a practical business perspective, it is on the wrong level. In their concern to avoid fiscal distortion the Commission has missed a significant opportunity to introduce a tax regime for Groupings at the EC level which reflects the underlying objective of the company law provisions.

Member Level Tax Issues

It is, of course, very easy to be critical of the Commission for failing to achieve the necessary harmony between the tax and company law objectives that would make the Grouping an entity which would really generate enthusiasm for cross-border co-operation within the EC, but ultimately the wording of the Regulation is a decision of the Member States and it is they who bear the responsibility not only for Art 40, but also for its effective implementation into their domestic tax legislation.

The framework for the taxation of Groupings was the subject of substantial discussions between the Commission and the Revenue Authorities from the individual Member States. From the very beginning, it appears that there was a substantial majority in favour of treating the Grouping as a 'see-through' entity although the UK Revenue Authorities are believed initially to have favoured a simple corporate form for taxation purposes.

Once the framework of taxation had been agreed and incorporated into the Regulation in 1985, the tasks of dealing with the necessary detailed work involved in implementing the Commission's objective and of ensuring that any new provisions relating specifically to Groupings were dove-tailed satisfactorily into national tax law, was left entirely to the national tax authorities of the Member States.

In the four years between the adoption of the Regulation and its coming into effect on 1 July 1989, few governments of Member States in fact introduced legislation to give effect to the Commission's intent. This was unfortunate as many individuals and companies who expressed an interest in the concept of the Grouping were unable to ascertain the implications of using this type of business entity.

Many countries still do not have legislation on the statute book. However, in the UK, the Finance Act does now lay down legislation on the taxation of Groupings. This was the subject of a consultation exercise begun with certain professional bodies and representatives of industry in the summer of 1989 and widened in January 1990 with the release of draft legislation in the form of a Consultative Document.

It is with the UK proposals that this section of the chapter is primarily concerned although issues relating to other Member States will be considered at a later point.

United Kingdom

The UK legislation is enacted through s 69 of and Sch 11 to the Finance Act 1990. The Finance Act inserts a new s 510A into the Income and Corporation Taxes Act 1988 (ICTA 1988) and two new sections (12A and 98B) into the Taxes Management Act 1970 (TMA 1970) together with some minor consequential amendments to other administrative provisions. The main part of the legislation, s 510A of ICTA 1988 is extremely brief, briefer even than the text in the Consultative Document, but it is clear that its brevity does not imply either a lack of interest or a failure to think through the complex tax issues which affect the interaction between the concept of the Grouping and UK domestic tax law. The legislation is brief because it has been neatly shoe-horned into the existing framework of law and practice and, in its form, it is very economical. However, for all its mastery of form, it is likely to be a piece of legislation which the layman will find difficult if not impossible to use, because, in the areas of greatest importance, it leans so heavily on existing legislation and Revenue practice and because, particularly in the international area, much of the framework for taxation is, and will remain unwritten.

It is worth reviewing the UK legislation in some detail, since it represents perhaps the clearest exposition of the way in which Groupings will fit into a domestic tax system.

Territoriality

The first, and fundamental point is that UK legislation will apply not only to Groupings registered in the UK but to UK source income of Members of Groupings wherever the Grouping is registered within the EC. A UK member will, therefore, be subject to the provisions of Sch 9 of the Finance Act 1990 in the same way, whether the Grouping itself is registered in the UK, France, Germany or elsewhere in the EC.

Application

Secondly, in drafting the legislation, the Inland Revenue followed closely the terms of Art 40 of the Regulation by making it applicable only 'for the purposes of charging tax in respect of income and gains'. The Finance Act 1990 does not, therefore, make any specific provision with regard to withholding taxes, Stamp Duty, PAYE or the Sub-Contractors' Tax Deduction Scheme and HM Customs & Excise have indicated that no special legislation is necessary on Value Added Tax.

Nature of Grouping

The Finance Act 1990 accepts that there are likely to be two forms of Grouping, namely a Grouping which does not carry on a trade or profession but is merely supportive of its Members' activities (effectively a cost centre) and one which does conduct such a trade or profession. Of these, they consider that the former will represent the vast majority. It will be interesting to see if that is the case. The test which will be applied to determine the appropriate characterisation will be the familiar test developed in case law.

Where no trade or profession is carried on, the Finance Act 1990 treats expenditure incurred and any income received by a Grouping as incurred or received purely as the agent of the Member, such that for a UK Member of a UK registered Grouping, the expenses and any income will be treated as if incurred by the Member itself. On this basis, the normal UK rules will apply to determine whether those expenses are deductible. Where capital expenditure is concerned, new s 510A(3) of ICTA 1988 will, by treating the Member as owning its share of the assets of the Grouping directly, entitle the Member to claim whatever capital allowances are available on that expenditure.

Where the Grouping does carry on a trade or profession, it is regarded, for the purposes of charging tax in respect of income and gains, as a partnership of the Members of the Grouping.

In broad terms, this means that most of the issues identified in the previous section will arise in the case of a UK Grouping. There will also be a number of issues which are unique to the UK.

Loss relief

One of those issues is the direct result of Groupings being brought within the existing partnership legislation, largely unamended. Where a Grouping, which is controlled outside the UK, carries on a trade or profession outside the UK, the effect of s 112 of ICTA 1988 will be that those activities will be treated for UK tax purposes as giving rise to Schedule D, Case V income in the hands of a UK Member. As far as the UK Member is concerned, this appears to apply irrespective of whether the Grouping is registered in the UK or another Member State. Correspondingly, any losses incurred in those same activities will be treated as Case V losses and not, therefore, available for general offset against profits or gains but only against Case V income. This is an unfortunate result and is a problem not generally encountered elsewhere in the EC. It may act as a disincentive to UK companies to become involved in Groupings.

Ownership of assets: capital gains tax

With regard to the ownership of assets, s 510A(3)(b) of ICTA 1988 makes it clear that for UK tax purposes, each Member will be regarded as owning a share of the Grouping's assets and sharing its liabilities. The shares will be determined in accordance with the contract under which the Grouping is established as required by s 510A(4) and (5). Where shares in property rights and liabilities are specified, those shares will form the basis for taxation purposes. Where asset sharing ratios are not specified in the contract, profit sharing ratios will be used and if those are not specified, the Members will be assumed to share assets and profits equally.

The effect of this proposal, specifically spelled out in the draft legislation, is that a Member of a Grouping will be treated, for capital gains tax purposes, as acquiring or disposing of an asset whenever the Grouping itself makes such an acquisition or a disposal. The acquisition or disposal will be of the member's share in the asset, as calculated by reference to the appropriate ratios.

Similarly, whenever a Member joins or leaves a Grouping, and whenever there is a change in asset (or profit) sharing ratios, the Members will be treated as making an acquisition or a disposal.

A number of points arise from this analysis.

Changes in asset-sharing ratios

First, with regard to changes in asset sharing ratios, Inland Revenue have confirmed that they will apply Paragraph 4 of the 1975 Statement of Practice in the same way in the context of a Grouping as for a partnership. This will enable such changes to be effected without giving rise to an immediate capital gains tax cost to the extent that there is no direct payment of consideration outside the partnership and no adjustment, such as a revaluation of assets, in the partnership accounts. The application of this Statement of Practice will mitigate the effect of changes in the membership or asset/profit sharing ratios of a Grouping.

Roll-over relief

Secondly, as regards the application of roll-over relief, Inland Revenue have now clarified the position. Their approach represents a logical extension of the existing roll-over relief regime. A UK Member, transferring into a Grouping an asset qualifying under ss 115 and 118 of the Capital Gains Taxes Act (CGTA) 1979 will be entitled to broadly the same relief as a UK trader making an equivalent disposal. He will be able to roll-over the gains into new qualifying assets acquired including his share of qualifying assets transferred into or acquired by the Grouping.

For example, two Members may each transfer into a Grouping appreciated real estate which they have hitherto owned and occupied for the purposes of their respective trades. A UK Member would be able to claim roll-over relief on his part disposal against his acquisition of part of the property transferred in by the other. This accords with the somewhat pragmatic approach which is taken by Inland Revenue to the requirement that the sales *consideration* for the old asset is *applied* in acquiring the new asset. In a case such as this, both the concept of sales consideration and the application of that consideration are a little nebulous.

In order to avoid confusion, Inland Revenue have said that where the Member concerned is a UK company, gains arising on transfers into or out of the Grouping will be capable of being rolled-over into acquisitions made by other members of the company's UK capital gains group.

The facility to roll-over gains in this way is very welcome, but it will not provide a solution to all the difficulties. It will often be the case that while one Member contributes assets, another will simply contribute cash, giving no basis for a roll-over claim for the first Member. Similarly, even where two Members each contribute assets, they may not all fall within s 118 of the CGTA 1979, leaving one of the Members with a tax cost on setting up the Grouping. This is an unattractive aspect of the UK proposals which may discourage full UK participation in Groupings. (It is submitted that a provision to defer any tax arising on the transfer of appreciated property to a Grouping would have given a more equitable result and have reflected more accurately the Commission's desire to encourage cross-border co-operation.)

Non-residents

As far as non-UK resident Members are concerned, the implications of the legislation are that, except where the Grouping is carrying on a trade or profession in the UK, the mere ownership of assets through a Grouping will not bring that non-resident within the charge to UK capital gains tax.

For the non-resident Member of a Grouping which is trading in the UK, the roll-over legislation will apply, but will apply in the more restricted way imposed by s 129 of the Finance Act 1989. The broad effect of this, in the context of a Grouping, would be that where the Grouping made a disposal of an appreciated UK asset, the non-resident Member would be able to roll-over his part of the gain only into new qualifying chargeable assets. He would be unable to roll-over the gain against the acquisition of assets outside the UK where they are outside the scope of UK tax. A UK Member would normally be able to roll gains over into non-UK situs assets because those new assets would be chargeable to UK tax in his hands.

Transfer of registration

Under the UK proposals a non-resident Member of a UK based Grouping might also be adversely affected by a transfer of the country of registration of the Grouping (specifically contemplated in Arts 13 and 14 of the Regulation). Inland Revenue have indicated that it will be a question of fact, under s 127 of the Finance Act 1989, whether the assets cease to be used for a UK trade or business and whether the deemed disposal provisions, therefore, apply.

It should be noted that under s 66 of the Finance Act 1988, a Grouping will be resident in the UK if it is registered in the UK for the purposes of domestic taxation (a point emphasised in the Inland Revenue Press Release of 19 April 1990). A change of the country of registration will therefore represent a change of residence. One of the implications of this is that a change of residence will require compliance with broadly the same procedures of notification that apply when a 'normal' company is emigrated. The Inland Revenue have said that the issue of specific guidance on this point is currently under consideration.

Incorporation

Finally, in the capital gains area, the Finance Act 1990 makes no specific reference to the position on the incorporation of a Grouping – an event which may well occur where Groupings are successful. The regime which will apply is, therefore, that which already applies to the incorporation of partnerships of individuals and of companies. For individual Members, the availability of a hold-over of gains is covered by s 123 of the CGTA 1979. However, there is no parallel legislation for a corporate Member. Where a Grouping with corporate Members is incorporated, any gains arising on assets transferred to the company will be taxable in the normal way. This is particularly regrettable as it will actively discourage the incorporation of Groupings for reasons which are difficult to discern.

Currency issues

One aspect on which the Finance Act 1990 is entirely silent is the treatment of currency issues. Given the current debate between the profession, industry and Inland Revenue on this area, the omission is not, perhaps, surprising. However, this is a subject which will need to be addressed in practice, bearing in mind particularly the compulsorily transnational character of the entity. It may cause particular problems where, in the UK context, a disposal of foreign currency assets could trigger a capital gains charge.

International tax

The UK legislation makes no specific reference to the treatment of Groupings by the Inland Revenue for tax treaty purposes. However, they have given some informal guidance on their position.

Inland Revenue accept that although a Grouping is resident in the UK for domestic taxation purposes under the provisions of s 66 of the Finance Act 1988, it will not be treated as a resident for the purposes of UK treaties which follow the OECD Model Treaty definition of residence referred to earlier in this chapter. However, some UK treaties do not follow this wording. For instance, the UK/Australia treaty defines a UK resident to include 'any United Kingdom company' and defines a UK company as 'any company [body corporate] which is managed and controlled in the United Kingdom and which is not an Australian company'. On this basis, a Grouping registered in the UK and managed and controlled there will be a resident for the purposes of the UK/Australia treaty. If it was not managed and controlled in the UK, the treaty would not apply. The wording of the UK/US treaty has similar implications. A resident of the UK is defined to include a corporation whose business is managed and controlled in the UK, which would again qualify a Grouping which was managed and controlled in the UK. Interestingly, Art 3(1)(b)(ii) excludes a partnership from the definition of a UK corporation but under the UK draft legislation on Groupings, a Grouping is not a partnership, even though the Members are, under s 510A(3)(b) of ICTA 1988, to be regarded as carrying on a trade or profession in partnership for the purposes of charging tax in respect of income and gains. However, the majority of UK treaties will not recognise the Grouping as resident in the UK.

Tax administration

In the area of administration, the Finance Act 1990 has introduced a number of additional points which were not set out in the Consultative Document, although precisely how this legislation fits together is not clear at present.

As far as the making of assessments is concerned, the new s 510A(7) of ICTA 1988 states that s 111 of ICTA 1988 shall not apply where the activities of a Grouping fall to be considered as a trade or profession, thereby removing the possibility that an assessment will be raised on the Grouping as a whole, but s 510A(8) requires that the profits of the Grouping on which the Members are subject to income tax shall be computed jointly, even though assessed separately. This seems to imply a joint return from the individual Members of a Grouping, but suggests a requirement for separate returns from corporate Members.

The position is, however, complicated by new s 12A of the TMA 1970, which empowers an Inspector, for the purposes of making assessments to income tax, corporation tax and capital gains tax, to require a return and accounts from the Grouping itself (acting through the manager or managers) or from any Member. At the time of writing, the contents of the return which may be required from the Grouping have not been specified and it is not, therefore, clear whether a UK corporate Member of a Grouping will meet its filing obligations in this way, or by way of the separate returns implied by s 510A(8).

The new s 98B of the TMA 1970 brings in the normal corporate penalties for failure to make the appropriate returns and for fraudulent or negligent misstatement and the minor amendments to ss 36 and 40 of that Act deem any such act or omission by any Member to be the act or omission of each Member of the Grouping. This is a very harsh provision, which could potentially affect a Member of a Grouping who has complied with all requests for information from Inland Revenue.

Inland Revenue have said in their Press Release dated 19 April 1990, that, as far as payments made by or to a Grouping with a UK Member are concerned, they will look through the Grouping and treat the appropriate part of the payment as made by or to the UK Member.

In this way, where a Grouping makes annual payments, the UK Member's share will be treated as a charge on income and, where relief for such payments is dependent on tax having been deducted by the payer, the tax deducted by the Grouping will be considered as tax deducted by the Member. Receipts by a Grouping which have been paid under deduction of tax will be treated as if they were receipts by the Member, which had suffered tax at source. Although not specifically stated in the Press Release, Inland Revenue will presumably apply these rules consistently in both the domestic and international context and will be prepared to grant treaty relief on that basis.

Inland Revenue have also indicated informally that they will look through the Grouping for the purposes of applying the permanent establishment concept. They do not consider that, in the UK, the Grouping will be left without treaty protection in that respect.

Where a permanent establishment is considered to exist, as noted above, the taxation position may be complex if the Grouping is funded on an interest bearing basis either by third party lenders or by funds provided by the Members themselves. Inland Revenue have said informally that, in most situations, they will not seek to use a free working capital or thin capitalisation argument to restrict the deductibility of interest incurred in connection with the activities carried on by the Grouping, for UK taxation purposes. They have, however, reserved the right to look at individual situations which they may regard as abusive. They have also said that, in the case of a UK registered Grouping, interest payable by the Grouping to one or more Members in respect of funds provided, will be normally treated as deductible against the taxable profits as computed for the individual Members. This will presumably be subject to the application of the rules in ss 82, 338 and 340 of ICTA 1988.

A point on which there may still be some debate is how tax on non-resident Members of a UK Grouping should be enforced if direct assessment of the non-resident does not yield a payment of tax. From the Inland Revenue perspective it would be attractive, notwithstanding the disapplication of ICTA 1988, s 111, to be able to raise assessments on the Grouping as agent for the non-resident Members. However, the effect of this would be to make the Grouping (and ultimately the other Members) liable for the tax obligation of a defaulting non-resident Member. This is a very unattractive result and runs directly counter to the principle of fiscal transparency. Section 510A of ICTA 1988 does not entirely rule out the possibility, but it is perhaps unlikely to be pursued. Such a proposal could probably be resisted in the European Court of Justice.

Effective date

All the UK provisions are deemed to have had effect from 1 July 1989.

In summary, the UK legislation follows closely the approach taken by the Commission on the taxation treatment of Groupings. It is commendably brief but, as noted above, it will be difficult for non-tax specialists to work with because it relies so heavily on existing but scattered legislation for its real impact. It is easy to understand that Inland Revenue might be unwilling to set a precedent by issuing a Statement of Practice covering the taxation of Groupings in the UK, but it is to be hoped that, in time, they will devote resources to issuing an official booklet on the subject.

The main criticism which can be levelled at the UK legislation is not, however, its obscurity. It is that it provides little in the way of mitigation of the main taxation disadvantages which might arise from setting up and operating through a Grouping.

There are three main areas on which future lobbying by interested parties is likely to focus, with a view to making the use of a Grouping much more practical and attractive.

Partnership taxation

Reform will continue to be sought to eliminate at least the worst aspects of existing tax law on partnerships, such as the provisions on overseas losses. This could be a major task for the Authorities, but one which would have much merit.

Hold-over relief

There will undoubtedly be pressure on Inland Revenue to provide a hold-over mechanism in UK domestic legislation to defer gains arising on the transfer of appreciated property into a Grouping. There is nothing in the wording of the Regulation which would prevent this and it would be a logical and helpful step for those seeking to set up Groupings. It seems likely that appropriate safeguards against future loss of tax could readily be built into such measures.

Transfer taxes

A number of countries have seen the necessity to mitigate the transfer tax cost of transferring assets into a Grouping as part of setting up a joint venture. Again, this type of relief could be introduced relatively easily into the legislation and it is likely that there will also be lobbying in this area.

It is to be hoped that some of these proposals will eventually find their way into UK legislation, but this will clearly depend on the will of the government to encourage the use of this type of legal entity.

It is beyond the scope of this chapter to consider in similar detail the taxation treatment of Groupings registered or operating in other Member States. However, the concept of a Grouping is an international concept and the legal framework provided by the Regulation imposes a compulsory cross-border element which will necessarily involve the interaction of tax systems in more than one Member State. It would, therefore, be inappropriate to leave the taxation area without addressing, at least in outline, some of the main features of the taxation of Groupings in Member States other than the UK.

In theory, the mandatory nature of the Regulation should create much common ground between the taxation of Groupings in the individual Member States. Many Member States have some concept of a business partnership and the regime for Groupings is likely to be broadly based on the taxation treatment of such entities. In most Member States, Groupings will not be resident for treaty purposes, because of the influence of the OECD Model, but they may be treated as resident for domestic taxation purposes in some jurisdictions. Most will treat them as constituting a permanent establishment of their Members in the State in which they are registered and operate, except where the Groupings have very limited functions. As indicated above, there is already a debate on this issue in a number of countries and this seems likely to continue. Most Revenue Authorities will look through Groupings in applying withholding taxes and determining treaty benefits. A tax on the repatriation of the profits of a Grouping to its Members would seem to be ruled out by the application of the principle of fiscal transparency. For indirect tax purposes, it seems likely that all States will treat them as 'normal' business entities, entirely separate from their Members. Some are, however, likely to provide reliefs in the transfer tax area. Payroll and other taxes will apply as usual for any incorporated or unincorporated business. Wealth taxes will be in point in a number of jurisdictions.

Given this general consensus, it is probably more important to highlight the differences that exist between the treatment adopted in different States rather than to comment on the similarities. This text will, therefore, concentrate on any significant unusual features in individual States, on the debate that has occurred on the taxation treatment, in particular countries where that has been especially significant, and on the present state of tax legislation or stated practice, as a number of governments have yet to introduce even draft proposals for the taxation treatment of Groupings in their own jurisdiction.

At the time of writing, the position is as follows.

Belgium

The Belgian authorities introduced a law on 12 July 1989 to integrate the concept of the Grouping into Belgian law. Under that law, a Grouping is regarded as a legal person for all purposes except that of Belgian income tax.

Groupings will not be considered to be residents of Belgium for most tax treaties, although the Belgium/France treaty is an exception in this respect.

Most Groupings registered in Belgium will be regarded as forming a permanent establishment unless their activities can be relieved under the 'preparatory' or 'auxiliary' concept. However, opinion in Belgium has focused on the likelihood that this test will not be met because, in most circumstances, a Grouping will be carrying out its activities for the benefit of more than one enterprise.

Most Belgian treaties follow the OECD Model to the extent that interest incurred and borne by a permanent establishment in Belgium is deemed to have a Belgian source. As a result, it is likely that interest paid by a Grouping to a non-resident will be subject to withholding taxes. As from 1 March 1990, the basic rate of withholding is 10 per cent, which may be reduced under certain treaties.

The Belgian authorities have recognised the need for some mitigation of the transfer duties on the contribution of assets by a Member to a Grouping and on the return of those assets to the Member whether on leaving the Grouping or on its dissolution. The transfer of real estate from a Member to a Grouping as a contribution of capital will be free from transfer duty. This provision is incorporated in Art 12 of the law of 12 July 1989.

Under Art 13 of the same law, the remuneration of the manager of a Grouping is excluded from the charge to VAT.

Denmark

Legislation on Groupings was introduced to Parliament in Denmark in December 1988 and adopted on 30 March 1989. However, that law does not deal with the taxation issues.

The Danish Ministry of Taxes has indicated that the application of Art 40 of the Regulation will require Groupings to be treated as partnerships under Danish tax law.

Denmark levies no withholding taxes on interest and the application of Art 11(5) will not, therefore, be in point.

The acquisition of an interest in a Grouping is regarded as an acquisition of assets under Danish law and, similarly, when a Member leaves a Grouping, a disposal takes place.

Wealth tax may potentially apply to individuals who have an interest in a Grouping based in Denmark.

France

Legislation on Groupings was adopted in France on 13 June 1989.

The basic concept of the Grouping is closely modelled on the existing French form of Grouping known as a Groupement d'Interet Economique and, as such, follows closely on its taxation treatment.

In France, the profits or losses attributable to the Members will be calculated without allowing a deduction for interest payable to a Member of the Grouping.

The normal indirect tax regime will apply to Groupings based in France. In particular, transfers of property into a Grouping will be subject to the normal transfer duties which, in some cases, are as high as 14.2 per cent of the capital value transferred.

Germany

No legislation has been introduced in Germany dealing specifically with the taxation aspects of Groupings. However, in a letter dated 15 November 1988, the Federal Minister of Finance issued guidance on the taxation treatment.

The broad intention within German law is that a Grouping is to be treated as a partnership. However, there has been substantial debate in Germany as to whether a Grouping can have a profit motive and can, therefore, be subject to business taxation. This debate is reflected in the Minister of Finance's letter. In certain circumstances, a Grouping may not be subject to corporate income tax in Germany. However, where a profit motive can be identified, the Members will be taxed on their proportionate share of the profits or losses of the Grouping. This will always be the case where the Members of a Grouping are companies.

There has also been some considerable debate over whether a Grouping should be subject to trade tax on income and there have been conflicting reports about the likely outcome of this debate within the German government. The debate comes at a time when the trade tax itself is under review.

As far as indirect taxes are concerned, the normal regime will apply with the exception that the contribution of capital to a Grouping will not be subject to tax.

For the purposes of tax treaties, the German authorities will regard Groupings as meriting the same treatment as partnerships.

Greece

The taxation position of Groupings in Greece has still to be clarified. No legislation has yet been introduced.

Ireland

Ireland has introduced company law regulations to bring Groupings within the Irish legal system and the taxation position has been clarified in the Finance Act 1990. Section 29 of the Act broadly provides for Groupings to be treated as partnerships and thus brought within the existing framework of taxation for partnerships in Ireland. Assessments will be issued on the Members rather than the Grouping itself. The legislation is deemed to have been in effect since 1 July 1989.

Italy

No legislation or regulations have yet been introduced on Groupings in Italy, to deal with either the company law or taxation aspects.

Luxembourg

No legislation has been introduced in Luxembourg to deal with the taxation position of Groupings. However, a Government circular dated 3 February 1989 made some comment on the taxation issue. It indicates that the Members of a Grouping will not be subject to corporate tax in Luxembourg but will be subject to municipal tax to the extent that the Grouping is registered in Luxembourg and carries on its activities there.

The Netherlands

The Dutch State Secretary for Finance has indicated that no specific legislation is likely to be forthcoming to deal with the taxation treatment of Groupings in the Netherlands. However, detailed guidance notes were issued on 1 March 1990 which address most of the key taxation issues.

Under basic principles in the Netherlands, taxation will be levied on the Members of the Grouping on the basis of the profit sharing ratio set out in the contract governing the Grouping, or otherwise equally. The agreed profit allocation should meet arm's length principles.

A Grouping based in the Netherlands will not be considered to be a Dutch resident for treaty purposes. However, the Dutch tax regime does not normally require withholdings on interest or royalty payments and there are, therefore, unlikely to be withholdings on such payments if they are made by a Grouping.

A Grouping registered in the Netherlands will not itself be subject to the provisions of the Corporation Tax Act 1969 and a Grouping will not, therefore, even in the limited circumstances in which a holding of shares is permissible, be able to qualify for the substantial holding (participation) exemption in respect of any shares it may hold. However, a Dutch member of a Grouping could qualify for that exemption on a look-through basis. The Dutch State Secretary for Finance has indicated that the authorities in the Netherlands intend to adopt the narrow interpretation of Art 5(4) of the OECD Model Treaty, so that even where a Grouping carries on activities which are of an auxiliary or preparatory nature, it will be considered a permanent establishment of its Members because it serves more than one enterprise. The Members will, therefore, always be potentially taxable in the Netherlands, presumably on a mark-up or other agreed basis, where the Grouping makes no actual charge for its services.

A Dutch Member of a Grouping based outside the Netherlands will be treated in a similar way to a company with overseas activities. Where the overseas activities constitute a permanent establishment, the Dutch Authorities will apply an exemption from Dutch tax on the Member. Where they do not constitute a permanent establishment, the results will be fully taxable in the Netherlands.

The normal indirect tax regime will apply to Groupings in the Netherlands. However, the transfer of assets into a Grouping by way of capital will not be subject to the normal capital tax.

A natural person, resident in the Netherlands, may be subject to the provisions of the Wealth Tax Act 1964 in respect of his interest in a Grouping.

The conversion of a Grouping into a co-operative association will give rise to a charge to income tax or corporation tax on the difference between the book and market value of the business transferred to the new entity. However, proposals to provide exemptions from this charge will be introduced at a later date. No other taxes, including transfer taxes, will arise on the conversion.

Portugal

Under the Portuguese Corporate Tax Code, the profits or losses of a Grouping will be computed by the rules applicable to companies and directly imputed to each Member of the Grouping in proportion to their interest in it. Taxation will then be applied in accordance with the status of the Member as a resident, non-resident, individual or company. However, there is no specific legislation yet on this subject.

Spain

The basic principles of the Grouping are not new to Spain and the tax law which will apply to Groupings is broadly based on earlier legislation.

The profits or losses of a Grouping based in Spain will be taxable only in the hands of the Members, where they will be aggregated for Spanish tax purposes with their other taxable profits or losses. The interests of non-residents will be treated in the same way as permanent establishments of non-residents.

The normal indirect tax regime will apply to Groupings constituted in Spain, subject to certain reliefs. In particular, 99 per cent of the normal taxes payable on the formation or dissolution will not apply in the case of a Grouping. There will also be special reliefs for Groupings with activities in certain parts of Spain.

Under Spanish law, the administrators of Groupings in Spain will have the sole responsibility for making a tax return to the authorities.

There is clearly some way to go before all of the Member States have introduced appropriate legislation to incorporate Groupings into their domestic taxation framework. Most countries were slow to address the basic issues and slower still to consider the more complex problems to which the concept of the Grouping gives rise. To their credit, a number of countries have now given serious consideration to those issues but in most the position is still very far from clear.

The Future for Groupings

It is tempting to say that the future for Groupings must be brighter than the present because the present is so beset with uncertainty and confusion. This is undoubtedly the case and it would be difficult for any adviser to provide as certain an opinion on a structure involving a Grouping as he can currently give on a corporate or partnership structure.

The transition from concept to reality has been a peculiarly difficult one as far as the fiscal aspects are concerned. In most cases, too little attention has been given too late to putting into effect in domestic legislation the broad proposal which was agreed at the EC level before the passing of the Regulation in 1985. However, the period of uncertainty is now moving perceptibly towards its end and there seems a real likelihood that most of the Member States will soon have in place a recognised approach on Groupings so that firm advice can be given to prospective users of the Grouping concept.

The real issue is whether there will be a significant number of users and one of the key factors in the determination of that issue will undoubtedly be the final shape of the taxation regime that is introduced across the EC. There are many people who are interested in using Groupings both in industry and in the professions. There are many outside the EC who are looking closely at the Grouping as a business entity and are seeking ways to participate in them through existing EC vehicles. At the simple end of the scale, there are many potential users for whom the taxation regime for Groupings would not be a significant deterrent. With careful management, provided that the operations do not become too complex and do not involve transactions in the main areas of difficulty, there should be no significant adverse consequences.

There are undoubtedly ways of planning around the difficulties. Asset transfers may be costly in tax terms but it will often be possible to avoid them by leasing the assets out at a market rental. Withholdings may sometimes make this process less attractive but, on a case by case basis, it will often be possible to plan around them or neutralise their impact.

It should be possible in most situations to fund a Grouping without withholding tax problems on interest payments. Each case will always need careful attention but the problems will rarely be insurmountable. Third party borrowings will always be easier to manage than connected party funding.

The main difficulties lie where operations are complex and a Grouping is being used for a major business activity. It will always be difficult to manage the taxation position of a Grouping which has operations in several countries, especially where some of those operations are outside the EC. Similarly, it will always be more difficult to manage the withholding tax position where a Grouping is receiving or making a significant number of interest or royalty payments cross-border.

It is fair to say that much of the complexity could have been avoided if the Commission had put forward a simple corporate form for the Grouping, but that was not the will of the Member States. Some of the difficulties might not have arisen if it had been possible to legislate more fully at the EC level so that some of the taxation anomalies were eliminated at that point under the terms of the Regulation and not left for the individual Member States to address. However, the governments of the EC countries on whom the responsibility for levying taxes rests, appear collectively to have taken the view that the Grouping should be no more attractive a concept in its basic form than existing methods of cross-border co-operation. There does not appear to have been sufficient political will to ensure the introduction of a taxation regime for Groupings which would fully respond to the company law initiative for creating co-operation across frontiers.

It is the middle ground which has been lost. There is no doubt that the Grouping concept can even now be used by companies and individuals with simple co-operative ventures in mind. At the other end of the scale, there is no doubt that the concept of the Grouping will ultimately be used by creative investment banks and their advisers for large ventures where the specific nature of a Grouping allows them to achieve what could not be achieved in any other business form. The combination of tax transparency and potential off balance sheet treatment will look very attractive in some situations. However, in between those two, there will be a large number of companies and individuals who will be attracted initially by the concept of a Grouping but will find that, in practice, there are a great many taxation obstacles. Careful planning will remove some but not all of them.

It is for those companies, who would seem to be the natural target of the Regulation, that the present legislation is a disappointment. If the concept is to attract them, there will have to be changes at the national level to ensure that the process of co-operation across borders through a Grouping is no less attractive for a company than carrying out the same activity by itself. Until that point is reached, there is a danger that much of the energy of those who sincerely wish to co-operate will be diffused in the effort of finding an acceptable way through the tangle of legislation.

CHAPTER FIVE
IDENTIFICATION OF PROSPECTIVE COLLABORATORS

Introduction

This chapter is an investigation of the types of information required in the identification of prospective EEIG collaborators. It discusses the publicly available sources of information which the businessman can reasonably expect to be used to facilitate the identification process. The sources will be identified and objectively evaluated on the criteria of timeliness, usefulness and language.

To aid the identification of a suitable collaborator the following areas will be investigated.

(1) Researching an industry sector:
  (a) to identify the players from a set of predefined criteria;
  (b) to evaluate the state of the industry.

(2) Researching a named company:
  (a) to identify the culture within which it operates;
  (b) to identify its strategies, both historical and future;
  (c) to cover recent events in the history of the company.

Advice will be given on sources of help available to the businessman, covering libraries, government agencies, information brokers and consultants, company formation and search agencies.

The Research Process

It may be appropriate to ask a fundamental question at this stage as to why business information should be gathered at all. If a decision has been made to form an EEIG then surely business contacts could be requested to come up with some names, or the sales force requested to identify potential collaborators?

The reasons for not following this line of enquiry are many. It is neither strategic nor planned; nor is it discreet. The answers will already be known to the businessman and are likely to be judgmental and subjective. Colleagues and employees are valuable sources of information – they should not, however, be the only ones. Research into companies and industries will provide a wider range of names for consideration. Business and financial performance can be evaluated from press stories, market and annual reports, and product lines can be identified from published directories. Properly planned and systematically executed information gathering makes the whole job more efficient and leaves the businessman free for the effective running of his current business.

It is recommended that a librarian, information specialist or researcher be employed to carry out the work. The alternative is worthy of consideration. It is unlikely that the businessman could do the work himself and run his business at the same time. Nor it is likely that he could do the research himself in terms of knowledge of published sources, linguistic ability, and technical expertise to access electronic databases which are required. He will not have the time to find the correct library which holds the directory needed, visit the library, or make photocopies of the relevant section. This can all be done *for* him and, combined with analysis of the results, to greater effect than that achieved by his own efforts. Information professionals are trained in information sources and are usually curious people by nature.

The European Dimension

Doing business in Europe is different – both in terms of language and culture. The British still have a poor reputation for linguistic ability, although the popularity of evening classes in foreign languages and the proliferation of crash language courses both here and overseas is testimony to the awareness of these deficiences and an attempt to overcome them. The Scandinavians speak excellent English on the whole but it can vary a great deal in other countries. It should be remembered when telephoning a company overseas that the switchboard operator and the secretary are unlikely to speak English.

The cultural differences between the UK and its European neighbours are as many as there are countries. It should generally be remembered that information is not given as freely as in the UK. Reporting requirements for company financial information in Europe are minimal, particularly for small companies. In addition to the research carried out in the UK it may be necessary to undertake field work through a network of investment bankers, brokers or other external advisers. There are also difficulties in ensuring the quality of the information available with reference to standards of accounting, auditing and reporting. The ability to understand fully the financial situation of a company may prove difficult and so other sources are used to give as complete a picture as possible. There are very few short cuts to finding basic information on companies or markets.

Working hours and holidays differ as do styles of management. Recognition should be given to both the intangible (national tastes and cultural prejudices) and the tangible (regulations and transport problems).

Coverage

It is necessary to view the widest possible range of sources, including annual reports, company documents, trade literature, journal and newspaper articles, market reports, brokers' notes and statistics, to ensure coverage is as complete as possible. It will be apparent that many information sources can now be considered pan-European in scope. The media in which these sources are available – paper, microform or electronic – are identified. Reference is made to them in the course of this chapter and the reader can find fuller details in Appendix III which includes other sources of interest which are not discussed here.

It is assumed for the purposes of this discussion that the entity seeking to form the EEIG will be a company and this assumption influences the sources of information outlined here. Information on government agencies or partnerships is very limited and therefore omitted from this discussion. It is intended to show what can be expected to be found so that unrealistic expectations do not hinder the information gathering process. It is reasonable to assume that company names, locations, product lines, and financial performance can be identified. Information on personnel, the markets served and an external evaluation of the company's performance is also normally available. It is, however, important to know when to stop looking. At the end of this chapter there is a section on how to tackle the research from an administrative point of view, and this covers timing, budget, prioritisation of work and output.

Researching an Industry Sector

Identifying the Players

The first task in researching and evaluating an industry is to identify the players from a set of predefined criteria. A decision is made as to the list of identifiable facts which each company should match, for example, sales turnover, location, product range, or number of employees. For sales and employee figures a decision is made as to whether the research will identify actual values only or whether an upper or lower limit is to be set (eg companies who employ between 50 and 100 people). If the only required criterion is that companies belong to a certain industry sector the researcher begins by scanning published directories relating to that sector. If the sector produces a European or International directory this is often a useful starting point.

Industry Source Material

To take an example in the chemical industry, titles such as the *World Chemistry Industry Yearbook* published by Chemical Data Sources, or *Chemical Research Faculties – an International Directory* published by the American

Chemical Society are useful. Chemical Intelligence Services produce *Chemfacts* which survey products and producers in Belgium, Germany, France, Italy, the Netherlands, Portugal, Scandinavia, Spain and the UK. Suitable partners in the computing industry may be traced through *Electronics Research Centres*, published by Longman, while those interested in the telecommunications sector should consider the *International Directory of Telecommunications*, published by Longman. A good directory which lists International/European sources of business information is an invaluable tool and a selection of these is included in Appendix III.

General European and country-specific company directories can also be looked at to identify further names and to fill in gaps in the criteria set. The directories mentioned here, or ones with similar coverage, are normally available in major public libraries.

Initial checking of source material will show at an early stage what is going to be easy to find and how up-to-date the available information is. The researcher will then know where to concentrate his efforts in order to fill any gaps.

Using industry-specific sources in published form has one serious disadvantage – there is no quick way to scan and select the information required. If the initial search is to establish a list of facts about the companies in the sector then access to electronic databases is valuable.

Throughout this chapter great emphasis has been placed on the use of electronic databases in the information gathering process. This is for a variety of reasons; speed of retrieval of data, flexible manipulation of numeric data into report or spreadsheet formats, and an overall greater availability of information electronically. These databases can be accessed by an information specialist already employed in-house or by contracting the work to an information broker or agency and is described in more detail below. It is not proposed to discuss how to access online databases or how to obtain the hardware or software necessary.

Electronic databases are not to be used exclusively, nor should published directories, which date quickly and are inflexible to use. It is emphasised that there is a need to combine all sources, each clarifying, verifying or complementing the others.

Carrying Out the Search Online

The search via an online database to draw up the list of companies in a given sector would be handled as follows. Having selected the appropriate file, the researcher will key in the chosen set of parameters and the computer will generate a number of 'hits' relating to the number of items on that file matching the specified criteria. The speed of search and retrieval of the data makes it easier and usually cheaper in personnel time than manually searching through directories. With manual information gathering the researcher is limited to sources physically available to hand. The researcher is further constrained by the quality of indexing in the directory which is being consulted. Online information providers make the retrieval process easier through the provision of searchable fields and controlled codes on the database. An experienced and knowledgeable searcher will get more out of the system than a novice, but developments in software programs and guides to the files provided by their producers help beginners formulate their search in such a way as to achieve a reasonable answer. It is important to note that for UK companies a wider range of criteria, especially accounting items, is available for online searching than that available for Continental European companies. For the latter, sales figures are sometimes available, but where not supplied, employee figures should be sought out as an indication of company size. It should be noted that database entries are not always uniform in coverage. If sales figures are available for some companies it should not automatically be assumed that sales figures will be available for *all* companies. It is again emphasised that the experienced researcher does not rely on only one source of information for his work. Each directory, card-service, or online database has its strengths and weaknesses.

To identify suitable companies as prospective EEIG collaborators, a search might be carried out on a file called *D&B - European Dun's Market Identifiers* which is available on the DIALOG host system. A search on privately-owned, non-UK, freight-forwarding companies with between 50 and 100 employees produces 284 companies. A list of the top 25, sorted in descending order of sales is reproduced below with sales shown in US dollars. Other items which could have been shown include company address, sales in local currency and the name of the chief executive. This search took 10 minutes to prepare, five minutes to execute, including the sorting and printing of the report, and cost $29.07.

D & B—European Dun's Market Identifiers

Company Name	Country	Sales US Dollars
Gerlach Offshore BV	Netherlands	2,310,000,000
Nedlloyd Aircargo BV	Netherlands	2,310,000,000
Damco-Van Swieten BV	Netherlands	2,310,000,000
Damco Maritieme BV	Netherlands	2,210,000,000
Muller Air Freight BV	Netherlands	1,230,000,000
Van Ommeren Amsterdam BV	Netherlands	1,110,000,000
Oceanfreight BV	Netherlands	345,000,000
Vda de A Fernandez y Hijos	Spain	290,000,000
Fracht Fwo Ltd	Switzerland	171,000,000

Company Name	Country	Sales US Dollars
Trafico Maritimo Y Terrestre	Spain	166,000,000
Slavenburg En Huyser BV	Netherlands	158,000,000
Berastegui Y Cia, Sen C	Spain	141,000,000
Vilar Transitos Y Aduanas, SA	Spain	107,000,000
Joaquin Davila Y Cia, SA	Spain	99,600,000
Consignaciones Transitos y Tra	Spain	66,400,000
Coma Y Ribas, SL	Spain	63,900,000
Buzzi & Cappellaro Spa Traspor	Italy	59,800,000
Barnatrans, SA	Spain	58,100,000
TNT Ipec Switzerland AG	Switzerland	55,200,000
Comercial Fornesa, SA	Spain	53,900,000
Tecn Asesores De Comercio Inte	Spain	52,200,000
Bergareche Ruiz, SA	Spain	49,800,000
Van Uden S Scheepvaart-En Age	Netherlands	44,000,000
Heinrich Hanno En Co BV	Netherlands	41,900,000
Transp Y Navegacion Ramirez Hn	Spain	40,600,000

The date of this search was 20 January 1990.

Additional Source Material

Other electronic databases are now considered. KOMPASS, part of Reed International, is one system which has expanded its online coverage of European companies. Many people are familiar with the range of directories of the same name. Once again, any type of searching to be done on a pan-European basis can be carried out more effectively via the KOMPASS database than by days of scanning through each of the separate country directories. The *European Companies Database* produced by Kompass Online provides company information in one file from the following countries: France, West Germany, Italy, Denmark, Norway, Sweden, Belgium, the Netherlands, Luxembourg, Switzerland and Spain. The emphasis of the database is on manufacturing, industrial and associated services sectors. KOMPASS is well known for its very detailed industry and product classifications which allow producers of very specific items to be found. This is a facility which producers of other online files do not offer. KOMPASS provides 12 indices from which selection criteria can be drawn. These include company name, country, director's name, sales, number of employees, and industry/product. Output may be printed locally or downloaded onto disk and many formats are available, including mail label generation and structured files for database creation.

Other files, each having their own coverage, sources and output, are available. These include the suites of files from *Hoppenstedt* covering Austria, Germany and Benelux; *ABC West Germany*; *ABC Europe*, which provides information on companies in 32 European countries; *Creditreform-Bilanzdatenbank*, which contains balance sheets and ratios of German industrial companies available in two files – *Coin* in English and *Finn* in German. *L'Europeene de Donnees* is a set of five complementary files on two million French companies with material sourced from the *Bottin Direct Qui Decide en France*, the databases of the French Chambers of Commerce and Industry (TELEFIRM and FIRMEXPORT/FIRMIMPORT), information from the *Journaux Officiels* (which record French company creations, liquidations or bankruptcies) and *Vininfo Entreprises* from the Chamber of Commerce and Industry of Bordeaux.

A useful source of establishing the ownership of a company is *Who Owns Whom* available as a set of directories on a continent-by-continent basis, or as a database through Pergamon Financial Data Services.

The value of the telephone directory should not be overlooked. *Europages*, a European Yellow Pages covers a wide range of industry sectors and companies within the sector. The public libraries of the London Boroughs hold wide ranging collections, and a guide such as *The Union List of Telephone Directories held by Central London Reference Libraries* records the holdings of five of the London Boroughs and the Cities of London and Westminster.

Sector-screening research via online databases has the advantage of collecting basic data with speed and without the knowledge of any third parties. An examination of the information gathered is used to identify companies which may require further investigation if they look of interest as possible collaborators and this is dealt with later in the chapter.

Researching the Sector

In the course of identifying prospective fellow Members of an EEIG consideration is given to the industry sector concerned. If the sector is the same as that in which the businessman currently operates then much of the market/sector data should currently be available to him. He will also have a clear idea of the state of the industry. If, however, the purpose of the EEIG is to tender for contracts, the Members of the Grouping may divide the obligations of any contracts among themselves with the EEIG acting as project manager. In this case, the other industry sectors involved will not be as clearly understood and a systematic process of research must be established to ensure that prospective Members of the Grouping are not later found to be wanting, either financially, technically or culturally.

Research into the sector will look at two different types of sources: news stories in local, national, foreign newspapers and magazines, and market reports produced by trade associations, market research companies or stock-broking houses.

News stories

Most business libraries provided by local authorities will have a good range of newspapers available for consultation – some may even have indexes – but reference to older copies may only be through microfilm. Similarly the main trade press journals should be available from the larger business library collections. Many such libraries produce a catalogue of their holdings which is usually free of charge. It is difficult to gain access to foreign language newspapers and journals, first, in terms of physical access if there is no easily available source in the UK and secondly, in understanding the language if the reader has no, or minimal, language skills. Translation services are available but expensive. It is recommended, as before, that a specialist is consulted to access news/journal material online into whatever aspect of the industry is of interest. An online search would scan a wider range of sources than those available locally and, in almost all cases, the information would be translated into English. This search would result in a print-out of informative abstracts to relevant articles. The complete text of the articles may be obtained via the local library either from its own stock or from the British Library Document Supply Centre. Articles may also be ordered online via the database producer. UMI/ Data Courier offer such a service and recent experience showed a total time of 15 minutes from phoning the request to their offices in Louisville, Kentucky and receiving by fax the two-page article required.

Good online sources of newspaper/magazine articles include the group of files available from Predicasts, especially *Promt* (Predicasts Review of Markets and Technology) which provides long, informative summaries of articles on market information, technology, company news, and legislation/government news which has an impact on industry. Other news stories are included in *Financial Times Company Abstracts*, *Moody's Corporate News – International*, and REUTERS *Textline*.

Consideration should be given to the growing number of industry-specific files covering news stories relating to that industry and giving access to, in many cases, the only electronic source of its trade press. Examples here would include, *Financial Times Business Reports*, available via DATA-STAR or PROFILE, providing information on the electronics, media, business, finance, technology and energy markets; *Insurance Abstracts*; *Electronic Publishing Abstracts*; *Coffeeline*; *World Textiles*; and *Artificial Intelligence Online*. The businessman cannot hope to keep himself fully informed of every development in his own sector and regular access to these types of sources will pay dividends.

Some titles are now available electronically prior to publication such as *European Chemical News*. *The Financial Times* is available electronically at 00.00 hours British Standard Time, which means that businessmen in the US can see today's first edition while most of the UK is asleep. A useful file to be aware of is *Infomat* which covers continental sources including 'Handelsblatt' and 'Les Echos'. In addition the Infomat company provides a range of alerting services to the business community and a tailor-made monitoring service can be established giving regular delivery of abstracts of newspaper and magazine articles to a pre-determined set of criteria and from a pre-determined list of sources.

The services listed above mostly provide abstracts to articles but databases are increasing the availability of full-text coverage of newspapers and trade-related publications. The PROFILE host system, owned by the Financial Times, offers a good range of these as does Mead Data Central's NEXIS. PROFILE covers such publications as *The Banker*, *Campaign*, *The Economist* and *SuperMarketing*. NEXIS provides, in addition to a wide range of newspapers, a Newsletter file which includes *Coal Week International*, *High-Tech Materials Alert* and *World Tax Report*. Specialist newsletters are also reproduced in Predicasts *Newsletter Data-base*.

It is to be recommended that any research requiring access to these text databases be done by experienced personnel as the costs incurred can be high if the novice user dials into an online system, then begins to check the codes to use or the output format best suited for the work in hand, or generally 'thinks online'. The dial-up online systems currently charge a per minute connect charge and a data cost for the information viewed on screen or printed. To overcome these technical barriers to accessing information it is expected that suppliers will provide their products as databases stored locally, usually on the user's own computer or as a CD-ROM product (Compact Disk - Read Only Memory), although this is still in its infancy for text databases.

These newer systems have the advantage of having few commands to learn to access the information and incurring no costs once the initial annual fee is paid. CD-ROM systems do not contain the most recent information as they are usually updated less frequently (monthly or quarterly) than the dial-up services.

It will be apparent to the reader by now that each source has to be considered in terms of timeliness of information, ease of use, and frequency of updating.

Alerting services: Information on companies or markets can be systematically collected via a press cuttings service. Costs can vary but most operate on a standard reading fee plus a per cutting charge. Such a service should be considered as it can be less expensive than individual subscriptions to the periodicals and newspapers. If the cost of these subscriptions, personal reading and clipping time is added together the use of an agency becomes an attractive proposition. The agency will cover many titles which can include small local newspapers which give prominence to stories not considered newsworthy by the national press. These could include interviews with company personnel providing detail on future plans and strategies, or proposals for new plant providing local job opportunities.

A similar service could be set up on an electronic database by keying the requirements, and if necessary, the sources into the database and storing them in such a way that each time the file is updated on the host service the system is triggered to carry out the search and deliver the latest information by post or electronic mail.

Market reports

Published market reports from trade associations give a good general overview of the state of the industry. The information contained in the reports is usually supplied by the members of the association and it is here that useful statistical information can be found. Companies are often concerned about the confidentiality in supplying figures and other related information for the preparation of statistics by trade associations. It should never be possible to identify a specific business from the statistics thus compiled. Government agencies also generate a great deal of statistical information and the range available is shown in *Guide to Government Statistics* published by HMSO.

It is also permissible for companies to exchange relevant market data when it is part of the creation of a common industry standard. This would be relevant in the information technology sector in particular. The European Commission requires that any such agreements to exchange data should be notified to them or be discussed with them to obtain informal approval in draft before any documents are signed to agree to such exchanges.

Market research reports produced by commercial market research companies provide useful industry data as the information is compiled from face-to-face interviews with the players in the sector. To gain timely access to these reports a company needs to be a contributor to the raw data gathered by the market research company. Other interested parties can purchase the report three to six months after date of publication. The prices of market research reports are very wide-ranging, from as low as £50 to as much as £50,000. Frost & Sullivan, based in London and New York, specialise in reports on industrial research in hi-tech markets. They have, in the past few years, published reports on image processing, communications equipment and opto-electronic components.

Indexes to published market research are available in large public libraries and include *Marketing Surveys Index* published by Marketing Strategies for Industry, *Market Research* from the British Library, *Marketsearch* by Arlington Management Publications Ltd, and *Published Data on European Industrial Markets* by Industrial Aids Ltd. Each lists published research on markets, products, industries and companies. The British Library publication refers only to the collection held in the Science Reference and Information Service in London. An indication is given in the British Library index if the document is available for loan from the British Library Document Supply Centre. Indexes to market reports and the full text of some of the reports themselves are also available online through the PROFILE host system.

Key Note Euroview reports published by ICC analyse the market trends and forecasts of an entire EC market such as retail food or European drinking habits. The reports contain an economic overview, studies of national markets and profiles of individual countries. These reports are economically priced and a useful overview to a market.

Marketing Information

Marketing information is of prime importance in the research process. An important aspect of marketing is culture and the culture in which other companies operate must be identified at a very early stage. There has been a good deal of development in the European marketing database field as US marketing databases paid scant attention to the European culture. What sells products in the US may not do so in the UK. HARVEST and MAID are two full-text systems with a UK bias which provide marketing information. HARVEST also provides an added-value consultancy service. *Euromonitor Market Direction* is a database of original international market research on a wide range of consumer markets. Of the five reports compiled on each title, four are on Europe; UK, France, Germany and Italy. Updated every six months, the reports cover such topics as market overview, source of supply, prices and margins, market size and sectors, and retail distribution and packaging. PURE DATA covers the main product areas (approximately 3,500) in manufactured goods for 76 countries providing numerical and forecasting information.

Stockbrokers' Reports

Firms of stockbrokers produce reports on companies (and their sectors) in which they make a market. These reports are sent to fund managers to assist them in their investment decision-making. It is extremely difficult for an individual to obtain copies of these reports which is regrettable as they contain useful, sometimes unique pieces of information. On sectors and industries the topics likely to be covered are growth prospects, effects of economic changes and major players. Brokers' notes are available electronically through *Investext* and *ICC Stockbroker Research* databases. An embargo is placed on the notes by the issuing stockbroking firm and means a delay of up to two months after publication before being electronically available.

Summary

Enough information may by now have been gathered to make further detailed investigations into specific companies unnecessary. The directories provide names and contact details, the news stories describe recent reported events and the market studies show potential industry growth and comment on specific company performance. The next stage may be to write to the companies with whom the businessman is interested in forming an EEIG and simply wait for the replies.

Researching a Named Company

If further investigation of specific companies is necessary this section describes how to go about it. The main sources of published company information are directories, card-based services, annual reports and press cuttings. Annual reports and press cuttings are also available in microform while online databases are available for directory information, articles in newspapers and magazines, annual reports and financial data.

Disclosure of Company Information

Research work must be undertaken to establish whether the company in question is public or private, and, if public, on which stock exchange it is quoted. Many countries have more than one exchange, and given that companies on the European continent tend to register on a localised basis, a small, obscure exchange may have been chosen by the particular company of interest. The act of listing on a stock exchange results in the production of interesting documents and any subsequent financing deals the company may undertake will require additional documentation to be filed. If a company decides to list on a stock exchange in the US these documents should be sought as the Securities and Exchange Commission (SEC) requires a considerably greater amount of disclosure than the UK or Continental European authorities.

Gaining access to the other national markets and partnership between companies set up in different Member States are two activities which are only possible if sufficient information is obtained about the companies operating in each of the Member States. Important information about companies must be disclosed and made available to any interested party. It is necessary to consider the harmonisation of company law throughout the Member States of the EC and the subsequent impact on the availability of company documents. It is important to note that information on companies is culled from the documents they are required by law to issue and the role of the European Commission is an important one in this context in setting a European standard which all Member States must reach. *Disclosure of Company Documents in the European Community* published by the accountants and management consultants KPMG is recommended as a clear guide to the filing requirements of companies in each of the Member States.

Company Law Directives

The First Company Law Directive was adopted by the Council of Members on 9 March 1968. Seven directives have been adopted so far and five further proposals have been made. This chapter considers briefly the impact of the First, Fourth and Seventh Directives.

The First Company Law Directive imposed certain disclosure requirements for all limited liability companies and thus Member States have adopted fairly similar procedures. It is difficult to establish how the Member States have implemented the various Directives; copies of the legislation for each country are hard to obtain and available often only in the original language.

The designated registry offices in each Member State hold documents relating to limited liability companies and are required to make them available. Subsequent to a document being filed a notice is published in the national gazette of the relevant country – the notice may be the full or part text of the document or merely a reference to it. Companies which are not limited liability companies are required to make their documents available at their own head office.

Although disclosure requirements have been standardised under the First Directive the filing system in each Member State varies enormously. Registries may be local or central, the information may or may not be available on a computer, copies may be available on different media, ie microfilm or microfiche.

The First Directive requires the following documents and notifications to be filed:

(1) The statutes and instrument of constitution (also known as the memorandum and articles of association) and, if amendments are made, the complete amended text of the instrument and statutes.
(2) The appointment, termination of office and particulars of the persons who are authorised to represent the company or take part in the administration, supervision or control of the company.
(3) At least annually, the amount of the subscribed capital where the instrument of constitution or the statutes state an authorised capital, unless any increase in the capital subscribed necessitates an amendment of the statutes.
(4) The annual accounts for each financial year. The document containing the balance sheet must give details of the company officials who are required by law to certify it.
(5) The notice of any transfer of the company's registered office.
(6) The winding up of the company or any declaration of nullity of the company by the courts.
(7) The appointment, particulars and powers of liquidators unless their

powers are expressly and exclusively derived from law or from the statutes of the company.

(8) The termination of the liquidation and its striking off the register.

The compulsory application of the fourth requirement (above) in relation to 'private' companies was deferred until the implementation of the Fourth Directive which was adopted in 1978. That Directive, in turn, allowed Member States to defer until 1985 the requirement for private companies to file accounts, provided that copies of their accounts (and auditors' report thereon) are available to the public free of charge at the company's registered office.

The Fourth Directive on company disclosure requires that both 'public' and 'private' companies prepare annual accounts and adds that the requirement for public companies to file their annual accounts at a public registry should be extended to private companies. It also specifies the basic accounting rules to be followed in the preparation of the accounts, the format the accounts should take and the minimum information to be included in the supplementary notes. Small and medium-sized companies are allowed to file 'abridged' accounts. Monetary limits are set to define a company as 'small' or 'medium-sized' in each Member State. The Seventh Directive relates to the preparation and filing of consolidated accounts and was adopted on 13 June 1988. Despite the work undertaken by the EC there are still considerable national differences between the administrative arrangements for the formation of companies. Corporate affairs are still regulated at national level and there is no EC Company Registration Office.

The information above is included only as an indication of the availability of company documents. The impact of any of this on an EEIG should be discussed with the relevant professionals.

With the acquisition of these documents an examination of the financial performance of the company can be made. Other items to be considered as 'fall backs' if financial information is lacking include employee figures, volume of foreign trade and market share data, traced through press stories, market reports and statistics.

There should be an awareness of the different legal forms of companies as this also affects the availability of information. These different forms are described in many publications, but worthy of examination is *European Company Information: EEC Countries* published by London Business School Information Service.

Information Availability

It is appropriate to clarify that the information sources dealt with in this chapter are publicly available. There *are* ways of finding information through industrial espionage but it is not the intention to enter this area of suspect, often unethical, and frequently illegal form of business behaviour.

The exchange of information often takes place at conferences, seminars and industry-related committees and readers should be aware that the supply of confidential busines information to competitors may be in breach of Art 85 of the Treaty of Rome. While it is good business practice to use intelligence gained in the planning of pricing structures and other business activities, the European Commission forbids the exchange of secret business information between competitors which enables them to co-ordinate their market behaviour. In the context of this chapter it is, therefore, unlikely that sources will be found which can supply this sort of information.

In January 1990 brokers' lunches which took place between UK listed companies' finance directors and City analysts and investors became a target of the UK Government in its continuing investigation of the investment industry. The Department of Trade and Industry sees these lunches as potential sources of insider information. A draft European Directive on insider trading is, at the time of writing, being considered.

The reader should not be dismayed by the list of types of information not available in the open market. This chapter shows the wide range and diversity of sources which *can* be exploited for company and industry analysis. Many of the sources discussed are available in public libraries, others are accessible for a fee, either paid directly to the suppliers or as part of a research service offered by an agency or information broker. The question of the cost of obtaining information is often raised by business people, but the price should be considered relative to the commercial value of the information received and the management time saved in the acquisition of the said information.

Company Directories

Country by country directories give location details, number of sites and basic product information for each company listed. For example Dun & Bradstreet produce *France* 30,000 in two volumes. This title covers companies in most sectors in France which have a leading position in their markets or a sizeable turnover. The first volume contains an alphabetical index of company names. The second volume arranges the companies by geographical location, the unit of division being the *Departement*. There is also a listing by business activity arranged by four digit Standard Industrial Classification (SIC) code. This volume concludes with a selection of ranking tables. A reasonable amount of directory and financial information is given on each company but it may not cover some very small companies in niche markets. International Business Development and the International Herald Tribune produce the *French Company Handbook* which contains two page profiles of 85 companies. The number of companies covered by each source, its date of publication and the date of the last accounts items for each company are important points to find out when examining a source for its suitability for use. The *French Company*

Handbook is limited in coverage – only 85 companies – and the last year of accounts given – 1987 – are in US dollars, although the previous years are in French francs. This does not necessarily detract from the quality of the information contained in the book – the researcher should merely be aware of what the coverage of each source is. For Germany the *Mittelstaendische Unternehmen* produced by Verlag Hoppenstedt & Co covers approximately 21,000 medium-sized companies, employing between 20 and 100 staff or which have a turnover of between 2–10 million Deutsch marks. Financial information is limited. Another Verlag Hoppenstedt product which produces more detailed financial information is the *Handbuch der Deutschen Aktiengesellschaften* which is a loose-leaf service. *Kompass Italia* covers 30,000 Italian companies in a three volume publication. The publication provides the usual detailed product information for which Kompass is so well known but minimal financial information – only sales and nominal share capital. The product indexes appear in Italian, French, English, German and Spanish.

Time should be taken to identify the main directories available for each of the countries in which your prospective EEIG partner could be found. Appendix III indicates further sources to be explored.

Multi-lingual dictionaries to help the businessman cope with language difficulties are usually weak in commercial terminology. *Lexique UEC* produced by the Union Européene des Éxperts Comptables Économiques Financiers covers accounts terminology in 10 languages.

These initial sources can be supplemented from any of those already outlined in the section on researching an industry.

Assessing Financial Performance and Credit Risk

Credit and financial information are used to evaluate the viability of a business transaction. Both types of information are available through online databases and although the data for each is originally collected for different purposes they are increasingly used interchangeably in company research. The main area of use for this information is in the establishing of credentials and evaluating credit risk. The respective members of the EEIG need to evaluate the ability of each member to fulfil obligations in a long-term project.

Credit-Rating

One of the major credit-rating services to be used here is *Dunsprint* provided by Dun & Bradstreet. This is an international online service giving access to company files in 74 countries worldwide. Users can have direct access themselves to the information or place an order for the search to be carried out by Dun & Bradstreet through their DUNSTEL service. Companies can be monitored on a regular basis if requested. Dun & Bradstreet obtain their information from banks, customers of the subject companies, by questionnaire and by direct interview with the company. The information supplied through *Dunsprint* is provided in the native language of the company but a recent innovation to the service is the ability to obtain an instant translation into English. Details of address, telephone number, legal form, lines of business, SIC codes, names of directors or partners, parent or subsidiary companies, company history and court judgments are also provided. The financial data includes three years figures from the profit and loss and shows any changes in capital structure. Historically, one of the problems in searching *Dunsprint* online was that seven different passwords were needed to gain access to the seven databases. This has now been changed to provide a 'global password'. Access to this, as to other directly-supplied Dun & Bradstreet products, is via a subscription of pre-purchased units against which information provided is charged and deducted.

Financial Performance

Annual reports

The information that a company issues about itself, either as a legal requirement or to keep shareholders informed, can be closely examined to look for pointers to its culture, and its historical and future strategies. Copies, or photocopies, of glossy annual reports are available from the companies themselves, from business libraries, through company search or credit rating agencies (such as Dun & Bradstreet, Jordans, ICC, CCN/Guardian, Informations Internationales or Disclosure), or via information brokers (such as FTBI, First Contact or Find/SVP). Each of these services varies in speed of reply and cost. The CIFAR International Annual Reports Collection is available in the UK through the Disclosure Demand Centre in London and paper copies of Annual Reports from the major countries of Europe can be provided. It should be remembered that the Annual Report is normally produced in the native language of the company but increasingly English language versions are available. Photographs in the Annual Report show plant and installations, product lines and members of the board of directors. The chairman's report describes activity in the last financial year and the strategic implications of such activity. An indication of any strategic decisions to be taken in the next year is also given if the company considers it appropriate to release such information. If the company under investigation is the subsidiary of a non-EEC parent there may be some difficulty in establishing the financial performance of that individual operating company through the practice of preparing consolidated group accounts.

Information from the Annual Reports of major European companies is extracted by Extel to provide the *Extel European Company Card Service*. This service is available as a subscription or cards can be purchased singly. Each company has two cards issued; the Annual and the News Card, the latter produced after a major newsworthy event in the life of the company (acquisitions, financing arrangements, board changes). An additional benefit to this service is that Extel has available, through its library, copies of the original annual reports from which the Extel card is drawn up. Extel endeavours to keep 10 years' Annual Reports, Documents and Press Releases on a company. The *MIRAC* (McCarthy Information Reports and Accounts) service has a number of European companies available and is available as a microfiche product.

Stockbrokers' reports

Just as brokers' notes indicate the overall performance and direction of industry sectors they also serve as good in-depth analyses of individual companies, especially if produced by the house which acts as broker to the company in question. An online search will identify those of relevance, on the *Investext*, *ICC Stockbroker Research*, and *Nexis* files. Copies of brokers' reports on European companies are available from ARK Information Services based in New York and London. This service collects analyst research reports on European companies from over 35 European brokerage houses with the advantage that the reports have been translated into English. ARK also can provide the collection of original language French company reports from DAFSA, a major French broking house.

Company specific pan-European databases of interest include *Europe's Largest Companies* produced by ELC International and available as an online file on PERGAMON FINANCIAL DATA SERVICES. ELC also publish the data as a directory which indicates the relative performance of companies by providing ranking tables based on sales, profits, and number of employees, amongst others. An alphabetical list of all companies included in the directory gives basic information including address, telephone number and so on. The ELC database covers over 25,000 companies and provides information on ISIC codes, profits, assets, number of employees and senior management. *Datastream* provides balance sheet and profit and loss information for the major companies in Holland, Germany and France. Stock market performance is also provided by *Datastream* for Belgium, Denmark, Holland, France and Germany. Datastream, created originally by the stockbrokers Hoare Govett, and now owned by Dun & Bradstreet, is aimed primarily at stockbrokers and dealers and the information provided may be manipulated via the software into various report formats, graphics and types of statistical analysis. *Disclosure Europe* contains descriptive and financial information on companies traded on the European and Scandinavian stock exchanges. Basic company details are provided as well as a five year financial summary, balance sheet and income statement.

Jordans provides access to French financial information through its CD-

ROM product *DIANE* (Disque pour l'Analyse Economique). Some 80,000 companies are covered, with growth anticipated to 110,000 by early 1990. A further 125,000 Belgian companies are also available with information supplied from the database of the National Bank of Belgium. German company information from Creditreform is also being made available from Jordans in the same CD-ROM format.

Identify the Strategy

Research can provide useful clues as to what a company is doing in terms of development of new products, direction of investment or internal restructuring. So far, business and commercial databases have been discussed but it is important to consider the information provided by the scientific and technical files. These files are, by their very nature, weighted in favour of technical pieces of information, but they may show the first mention of a new product, or a new application for an existing product. Details of new factories being built or plant being installed provides the first clue to a company's investment plans. This sort of information is found in the specialised trade press of the specific industry and again the power of electronic databases to scan vast quantities of data very quickly is fundamental. Two hosts of significance are ESA-IRS and ORBIT. They offer a wide range of files including *Artificial Intelligence*, (the online version of Artificial Intelligence Abstracts, a monthly journal on the business, economic and technical aspects of artificial intelligence and related technologies) *Merlin-Tech*, on electrical and electronic engineering and *RAPRA*, considered the world's primary database on the technical and commercial literature from the polymer industries.

Further insights into the culture and strategy of a company can be gained through interviews with senior personnel which are printed in newspapers and magazines. News and current affairs databases are of two types: 'full-text' taken directly from the source and 'bibliographic' where an informative abstract of the original article has been prepared.

The complete text of news stories on specific companies can be tracked through the *McCarthy Cards: European Service*. Fifteen European sources are covered with the major articles extracted. The service is available in paper form, cumulated on microfiche or available online via the PROFILE host. *Nexis*, a full-text database, was introduced in the UK in 1984 and has always been seen as heavily American in bias but its coverage of European sources is increasing. It provides many files of news and market research information which include company data. REUTERS *Textline* remains the prime source of news information and covers, at the time of writing, 45 continental European newspapers. The specialised industry databases included on Textline cover an even larger number of trade and industry publications.

News and Current Affairs

Further monitoring of news and current affairs can take place through press cuttings services available through many agencies as described earlier. Of interest is the *HWWA Institut für Wirstchaftsferschung* which covers about 70,000 companies worldwide with files going back to 1908. In the UK Premium Monitoring, The International Press Cutting Bureau, Newscan, or Press Express will provide general or tailor-made services. A more complete list of agencies providing this service can be found in *Advertisers Annual*. The new technology which has changed the face of Fleet Street has opened up opportunities for electronic press cuttings services. *E-Mail Alert* takes as its source the *Financial Times* loaded from midnight on the morning of publication onto the PROFILE database. Customers are requested to specify keywords relating to subjects or companies of interest and the computer searches the new material daily and sends the complete text of up to five articles where those keywords are found to the customer's electronic mailbox by 2am on the day of publication. If between five and 20 articles are found, the relevant paragraphs are sent; if more than 20, the customer receives the headlines only. Time differences allow customers in the US to read the *Financial Times* online before it is published in New York and their cuttings can be in their mail-box before they go to bed. At present this service is only available for the *Financial Times* and it will be interesting to see if the whole of the PROFILE database will become available in this way.

Newswires are found on *Nexis*, PROFILE or *Textline*. Newswires are essentially to provide information which is very recent and some services, such as Reuters, provide the information on a screen with no archive or retrieval features. The other hosts mentioned above capture the information and store it as part of the general suite of files available for searching on an historical basis. *Nexis* gives access to *The Associated Press* files from January 1977, amongst others, PROFILE includes *TASS* giving the official Soviet view on international current affairs and *Textline* equally has a wide range including those produced by its parent Reuters.

Management Information

At various points in the chapter, reference has been made to the 'culture' or 'strategy' of the company. This can be investigated by a study of the literature of management which is rarely limited to any particular area of industry. Management online services are bibliographic rather than numeric or statistical and the information that is found in these sources requires supplementing from news and company databases to complete the picture. There are three main management databases and regrettably two of them are American in orientation. These two are *Management Contents* and *Abi-inform*. The third,

Management and Marketing Abstracts is stronger in the UK and provides international coverage.

Through the formation of the EEIG is created what may be considered as a set of equal partnerships. The management skills needed to develop this concept may be quite different from those needed to run a group of subsidiary companies. The techniques of control and command must be replaced by those of discussion and consent. A search of the published literature may reveal articles or books on the different types of management techniques required.

As product development cycles shorten in the manufacturing industries, pressure is put on retooling and retraining times which will have an impact on costs and employees. To ensure this is smoothly dealt with by all parties in the EEIG it is important to ensure that there is a match between the Members' strategic objectives. In discussions with partners the objectives need to be clearly stated and there should be mutual respect and trust. The contribution of each partner and the benefits, accountabilities and responsibilities should be clear. Personal skills in cultivating friendships and recognising the independence of partners is important as is an appreciation of cultural differences. The circumstances of each of the partners may change and this should be accommodated.

Reading publications in management techniques can be supplemented by membership of an appropriate management association. The British Institute of Management (BIM) runs a series of workshops and courses on a wide range of management issues. The BIM also has a wide-ranging publications programme covering books, reports, papers and checklists. It has a Management Information Centre giving access to published and audio-visual material and a Helpline service providing direct electronic access to management information.

Important management information to have to hand is a list of working hours and public holidays relating to each country of interest. There are many sources of use here, including the World Public Holidays guide in the International Stock Exchange Diary, the *Europa Yearbook*, and *Reuters Country Reports*, the last two of which are discussed below.

Economic and Political Information

Some background reading of basic source material can provide considerable knowledge of the economic and political climate of the country under review, although published sources can prove to be out of date as anyone who tried to follow events in Eastern Europe through the Winter and Spring of 1989-1990 will testify. The *Europa Yearbook* is an extremely useful source of background information. In the latest edition the section on France has an introductory survey which includes details of the country's location, climate, language, religion, recent history, and public holidays. This is followed by a statistical survey, a guide to the government, the judiciary, the press, and other similar topics. The section on trade and industry gives a list of Chambers of Commerce and Industrial Organisations all of whom may be of use in drawing up a contacts list.

Evaluative, analytical studies on countries can be obtained through *Oxford Analytica*, a service which produces a daily briefing including an executive summary of key events worldwide. This system is downloaded onto the user's own computer's hard disk and builds up into a searchable database. Frost & Sullivan offer a different kind of service with *Frost & Sullivan Political Risk* as do Reuters with their *Country Reports*. The Frost & Sullivan service assesses 85 countries through a team of country specialists and each report forecasts the 18-month and five-year outlook for stability, conflict, financial matters, investment and exports. *Reuters Country Reports* provide data which is collected daily by Reuters correspondents. The service covers 'News', which is kept on the system for 90 days, 'Country Profiles', analysing the country's political, economic and social situation, 'Economic Indicators' with sources, a 'Government List' and a 'Who's Who index'.

Demographic information may become important in considering the location of a manufacturing plant. It is generally predicted that there will be a shift in labour-intensive industries to southern Europe to take advantage of lower costs and a skilled younger population leaving service and high-value specialisations in the northern countries. Population statistics are published by the Statistical Office of the European Communities (EUROSTAT) under the title of *Population and Social Conditions*.

Bank reports are available electronically on *Nexis*, *Textline's World Banking Abstracts*, *Infomat*, and ESMERK. These are probably most useful for an economic overview of sectors and companies and for in-depth reports on the financial state of a particular part of the world.

An additional source of interest may be WEFA, a databank for econometric forecasting with data on OECD, EEC and individual countries. The information provided includes exchange rates, monetary series, interest rates, prices and production, government financing, national accounts, international liquidity and international transactions.

As UK national companies move closer to foreign markets through the creation of an EEIG or indeed through any other form of partnership or alliance there will be a need for the political environment to keep pace. If anything, business is ahead of politics in internationalisation. British business must keep abreast of the political situation to ensure that the appropriate legislation is introduced to favour their requirements. The daily debates of the House of Commons and the House of Lords are recorded in *Hansard*, held by most large public libraries or available electronically through *POLIS* (Parliamentary Online Information Service). Information on forthcoming debates and committees is printed weekly in the *Financial Times*.

Developments in the European Commission can be monitored via the EEC directives. Electronically this information is available on *Textline*, and on PROFILE via the *Spearhead* and *Deloittes* 1992 files.

Business Culture

Personal experiences of travelling abroad will give an indication of the great differences in culture between the European nations. During a first business trip to Spain it may come as a shock to find that lunch does not begin until at least two o'clock in the afternoon and ends around four o'clock. It can often be a meal of some substance. The evening meal is rarely eaten before nine or ten o'clock pm. Entertaining is also carried on in restaurants rather than at home. Various publications on 'doing business in . . .' are published by the large accountancy firms and it is advisable for the prospective EEIG Member unfamiliar with local customs to consult such a publication. Details of the geographical location of prospective collaborators' businesses may be obtained from the equivalent to the Ordnance Survey map which gives a good indication of population density, location of manufacturing plant, accessibility of motorways, rivers or airports.

During the course of preliminary meetings between prospective EEIG collaborators each will formulate opinions about the other as individuals. It is perhaps appropriate to mention at this stage in the search for a prospective EEIG collaborator that there is inevitably an element of subjective judgment on the part of the individuals involved. After all the weeks or months of preparation and research, only they can judge whether they will be able to work together. If the right sort of professional information support has been used then the prospective EEIG Members should be as well-briefed as possible on the performance, make-up, product range, and style of the company. The information received in the course of the research process will have increased awareness of the sort of company required and will have reduced the risk involved in the final choice of collaborator.

Other Sources of Help

Government Departments

The British government through the DTI and the British Overseas Trade Board aims to help companies in their business activities in exporting and provides access to sources of information. The DTI has a range of market reports available and information on new titles published is available in *Business Briefing* published by the Association of British Chambers of Commerce. Reports mentioned in the issue for 26 January 1990 were: (1) a report on the catering equipment market in the Netherlands and (2) a report on the Belgian construction industry. *Business Briefing* aims to replace the much-valued and sadly-missed *British Business* which ceased publication in 1989. *Business Briefing* also covers draft Technical Regulations received by the European

Commission from Member States, and news items relating to business opportunities.

Assistance in the research process is available from many publicly-funded bodies which are either direct government agencies or academic institutions.

The Small Firms Service (Department of Employment) provides free information on any matter of interest to a small business. It also provides business counselling given by experienced business people. This service can also put the entrepreneur in touch with his nearest Local Enterprise Agency which also provides help for small businesses. The DTI issues a booklet *Introducing the Enterprise Initiative* which covers details of all the assistance available to companies to increase their competitiveness. Included are details of the Consultancy Initiative, the Marketing Initiative and a list of other support services available through the DTI.

The Export Initiative staff can give direct access to the British Overseas Trade Information Service database (*Botis*). This database contains information on products and markets, overseas agents, distributors and importers, export opportunities, promotional events, and an index to other published market information. Use of this database will give details of contacts who could be investigated as potential collaborators. Attendance at promotional events also gives an opportunity of meeting suitable companies. The 'Fairs and Promotions Branch' of the DTI can be of assistance here. There is also an online database called *Fairbase* hosted by DATA-STAR which gives details of forthcoming trade fairs and exhibitions.

The Export Market Information Centre (EMIC) is based in London and operates on a self-help basis with advice on which sources to use and how to use them. The *Botis* database described above can be accessed and the following source material is available for consultation: statistics on worldwide trade and production figures and import/export data; market surveys and research reports; bank economic surveys; and reports of overseas missions. Overseas trade directories on manufacturing, import/export firms, agencies, and service industries are used to identify competitors, potential customers or collaborators. Development plans outline the current economic state of a country and put forward its plans which give background data and specific market leads. These plans are available for loan to exporters. Overseas mail order catalogues are kept on consumer goods and a range of foreign dictionaries is held. A search service is available for selected commercial online databases.

Specific sales leads, published tenders and indicators of future market opportunities are available from the *Export Intelligence Service* based on the *Botis* database. Regional offices of the DTI give free samples and explanatory leaflets on this service. Telephone numbers are given in Appendix III. There are two ways to receive information from this service. The first is to state the products and markets of interest and each item notified to the service will be matched against those requirements. Notification of appropriate items will be sent by post, fax, electronic mail or telex. The DTI offers this service through *Export Opportunities Limited*. The second means of access is to search the database daily on the PROFILE host system. Prices of each of these services can be obtained directly from both suppliers.

Tendering for Contracts

Earlier in the chapter it was mentioned that one of the functions of the EEIG might be to tender for contracts. The European Commission advertises invitations to tender for public contracts on a daily basis. These are contracts which exceed a value of approximately £90,000. Many contracts are divided into lots or have possibilities of sub-contracting which would be an ideal opportunity for an EEIG. The information is available on the EC's database *Tenders Electronic Daily* (TED) and is the electronic equivalent of 'Supplement S' to the *Official Journal of the European Communities*. Tender notices appear in English and are available for all members of the Community. Under the GATT agreement, notices from Japan, USA and Canada are included for tenders which exceed £180,000. The file is updated on a daily basis by 11 o'clock of the morning of the day of publication and notices remain for six months before deletion from the file. A useful feature of the file is that the company which has been awarded a contract can be identified, as can the date of the award and the criteria used to make the decision. A company called European Contracts Information Service will scan the information on this database on a daily basis and give notification the same day of any invitations to tender which may be of interest. The subscription to the service includes free access to the resources of the European Documentation Centre where the company is located – Glasgow University Library.

Dun & Bradstreet also offer a gateway to this database and to their own Contract Information Database (CID) through *Dunscontract*. Suppliers can use *Dunscontract* to send messages directly via electronic mail to the government agencies who are advertising contracts on the service. The contracts advertised on CID fall outside the criteria of TED and include tenders which do not meet the EEC threshold of 100,000 ECUs and which are submitted by private contractors to advertise sub-contracting opportunities. Advertising on CID is free of charge for clients of *Dunsprint*.

Other Government Help

Government assistance is also available for specialist market knowledge. A Regional Office of the DTI will provide contacts with the appropriate personnel in their market branches, the Area Advisory Group or a commercial department specialist in a Diplomatic Service Post overseas. The *Market Information Enquiry Service* is also accessed through the DTI regional offices. Structured market research is provided through the *Export Marketing Research Service*. Free professional advice is given on whether market surveys are needed and how to get such a survey started. Financial support is often available for market research studies carried out overseas. The DTI makes available the services of an Export Development Adviser from its export unit. An adviser will determine whether an export programme would work for the client. If the client decides to go ahead, counselling and advice hours are made available at very low cost. These advisers work through the Regional Offices of the DTI or local Chambers of Commerce. Some of the services outlined here may be available in the research process of identifying potential EEIG partners.

Fuller details of all Government initiatives for overseas markets are available in the brochure *The Export Initiative*.

Co-operative Networks

Local business and technical co-operative networks exist which allow access to business and technical information held by organisations within the area covered by the network. One such network is HATRICS which has its headquarters in Winchester with other centres based in libraries in Dorset, Hampshire and Somerset. Members of the network agree to pool non-sensitive resources with others. The staff of HATRICS call on these resources and those held at major public and academic libraries to find a source for the information required.

Euro Info Centres

Euro Info Centres were set up through the European Commission to help principally small and medium-sized companies and provide information on marketing, regulations, finance and business start-ups. These centres exist in each of the 12 Member States of the EC. Information searches can be carried out culling material from case studies, expert opinion and reports on various aspects of the business activity under investigation. The Centres also organise and participate in business events (trade fairs, exhibitions, and seminars).

Financial Incentives and Grants

EPRC Limited is a company associated with the University of Strathclyde, Scotland and is an authoritative source of information on financial incentives in the UK and Europe. Their information services include online databases on financial incentives, publications and consultancy services. Two of the databases are discussed here.

The AIMS database holds three files: (1) financial incentives for industry, commerce and tourism, (2) news on changes to financial incentives, and (3) financial incentives for agriculture, forestry and fishing. The information is sourced from over 60 national and regional UK public sector organisations and EC institutions.

EUROLOC (Locate in Europe information retrieval system) also holds three files: (1) industrial assistance (2) statistical information relating to incentives, and (3) a news file. The industrial assistance file details schemes on offer to private sector firms in Europe available from national governments and EC institutions. The standard format of the database shows what type of incentive each entry is (grant, tax concession, soft loan), what the eligibility characteristics are (size of firm, sector, location), value of incentive, conditions imposed on recipient, application procedures and contact point for further information. EUROLOC's aim is to make comparison of incentives possible.

A recent report on business grants from the European Commission has been published by Hertis Information and Research called *Grants from Europe: a survey of current awareness services*. The report describes the grants available and which sources provide the information; print, electronic or organisations.

Methodology

Prioritising the Work and Setting the Timescale

It is helpful to the researcher if the pieces of data required are prioritised in order of importance to the recipient of the research. It should be decided if a set number of prospective company names is required, with information on each provided as it is found, or alternatively the companies may need to be ranked by a particular indicator (sales, employee numbers, closest product mix to the recipient's own) and in-depth reports produced on each. The decision taken will be reflected in the methodology employed by the researcher. A timescale should be established so that the researcher knows how long he has to prepare the work. This may limit the amount of work that can be done, therefore the timetable should be a joint effort between both parties. The timing of the task should be based on the following: initial checking of availability of source material; purchase of any sources not available through libraries; extracting data from source materials, both published and electronic; identifying and filling any gaps in the research; preparing the report in the format required; discussion and feedback. Lead-times are especially important for published sources as some are hard to find and take time to obtain. Included here are annual reports, product literature and any other sources not available in local libraries or via electronic databases. Information from government sources and trade associations should also be ordered at the early stages.

Budgeting

It is helpful to set a budget for the task although certain aspects of this should be re-evaluated as the work progresses. The budget needs to cover any purchase of source materials not available for consultation in a library, ie costs for database searches, photocopying and fax charges, fees for specialist personnel (information brokers, government agencies, commercial information services). It is difficult, especially for managers of small companies, to relate directly the costs of information to benefits received. The costs are not as great as might be thought and the agencies available to the business community which provide advice and research facilities at low cost through government funding have been described. The actual purchase costs of any items mentioned or quoted estimates for online searches (other than the one sample search) have not been included in this discussion as these become very quickly out of date.

Output

The presentation of work must be given due consideration. The researcher will want to prepare the work to as high a standard as possible. The decision as to the final layout should be made at an early stage as it will affect the timing and budget for the project. It is unlikely that the businessman will require a professionally published piece but the work should at least be typed up and properly collated. Advances in word processing and desk-top publishing packages facilitate a good quality product for a small outlay.

Conclusion

Business intelligence is a hybrid function of strategic planning and market research. Even today few companies are organised to collect and analyse information in a systematic way. This chapter has attempted to address the various information needs of a business in identifying a prospective EEIG collaborator. It has identified ways of conducting initial research into an industry sector to define suitable companies and has pointed to sources of information on the state of the industry itself and its future prospects. Further sources have been identified which provide additional information on companies themselves in terms of their financial performance, and recent newsworthy events. This chapter has also advised on services available to the business community to carry out all or part of the information gathering and basic analysis required. Government and commercial services have been identified which ease the burden on the businessman.

In conclusion, it has been shown that the value of research cannot be underestimated. It is the most important tool in providing companies with the competitive edge. Carefully planned, well-executed research contributes to the business intelligence with which the businessman must be armed to move forward in the formation of this new business concept – the EEIG.

APPENDIX I

Model EEIG Agreement, Notes and Check-list of Clauses

Set out below are some clauses in an example of an Agreement to indicate the type of matters which should be considered when constructing an agreement for an EEIG. It should be noted that the appropriate wording for the clauses and items necessary to include in the Agreement will vary according to the individual circumstances of each EEIG. It is quite possible that in specific circumstances only some items will need to be covered by the Agreement or that different views will be required. The style of drafting of any Agreement will depend upon the agreed requirements of all the Members in the international context. Wording to be used should be checked in the context of other national laws as appropriate. The publishers and authors cannot accept any responsibility for reliance placed upon the wording of these examples. In all cases the wording of any EEIG Agreement should be approved by professional advisers who are aware of the specific requirements of the EEIG and its members.

(The * followed by the information in brackets indicate where alternatives could be inserted in the clauses.)

THIS AGREEMENT is made the day of 19 between the Original Members and sets out the terms on which the Original Members agree to form and operate a European Economic Interest Grouping upon the terms and with the effects laid down in Council Regulation (EEC) No 2137/85 of 25 July 1985 on the European Economic Interest Grouping (EEIG) and Statutory Instrument 1989/638 The European Economic Interest Grouping Regulations 1989.

IT IS HEREBY AGREED AS FOLLOWS:

1. Interpretation

Words and expressions used in this Agreement have the meanings and effect given to them in Schedule 11.

2. Preconditions to the Agreement

2.1 The parties hereto agree that conditional upon the satisfaction of the following matters they shall proceed with this Agreement to form an EEIG:

2.1.1 that each party has full power to enter into and perform this Agreement;

2.1.2 that each party may be the Member of the Grouping in accordance with the provisions of Art 4 of the Regulation;

2.1.3 that each party has not charged its assets or undertaking (or part thereof) in such a way as to constitute a charge over its participation in or membership of the Grouping *(save as disclosed in Schedule).

2.2 If these conditions shall not be satisfied at any time subsequent to the signing of this Agreement and prior to the time of registration this Agreement shall be null and void save to the extent that each party other than the party in breach of any condition shall be entitled to recover from the party in breach of any condition all costs which they have incurred in preparation of this Agreement or in attempting to register the Grouping and all losses of any kind whatsoever which result from any failure to register the Grouping with all the parties to the Agreement as Members.

3. Agreement to Form the Grouping

3.1 The Original Members hereby agree to form a European Economic Interest Grouping with the name, official address, objects, Members, and duration set out in the EEIG Particulars in Schedule 1.

3.2 Each party shall bear its own costs in relation to the preparation and execution of this Agreement save as provided in Clause 3.4 below.

3.3 It shall be the obligation of   to arrange for and carry into effect all measures required for the registration of the Grouping so that registration shall take place not later than three months after the execution of this Agreement. The costs of such measures shall be borne by the parties equally save as provided in Clause 2.2 above and Clause 3.4 below.

3.4 Upon registration the Members may unanimously agree that agreed amounts of the costs of each Member in relation to the preparation and execution of this Agreement and all steps to register the Grouping shall be borne by the Grouping.

4. Funding and Division of Profits and Losses

4.1 The Grouping shall be funded by the Members and facilities for the Grouping shall be contributed and provided by the Members in accordance *(with the budget of the Grouping unanimously agreed by the Members) *(with Schedule) and in accordance with such further arrangements as may be unanimously agreed from time to time by the Members.

4.2 The profits of the Grouping shall belong to the Members in the proportions set out in Schedule 2.

4.3 The losses of the Grouping shall be borne by the Members in the proportions set out in Schedule 2.

4.4 On the winding up of the Grouping any assets available for distribution amongst the Members shall be distributed amongst the Members in the proportions set out in Schedule 2.

4.5 Each Member may periodically draw on account of his share of profits such sums as he may be required to pay in respect of any taxation assessed by reference to his share of the profit of the Grouping and such other sums at such periods as may from time to time be unanimously agreed by the Members.

4.6 Unless and until the Members shall otherwise unanimously agree if any annual accounts of the Grouping shall show that in the period covered by those accounts any Member drew in excess of his share of profits for that period such Member shall forthwith refund the excess together with interest thereon at the rate of   per cent per annum above the base rate for the time being of *(any leading bank).

5. Admission of New Members

A natural person company firm or other legal body may only be admitted to Membership of the Grouping by unanimous decision in writing of all the Members. The provisions of Schedule 3 shall apply to the taking of any decision to admit a New Member.

6. Cessation of Membership

6.1 Any Member may cease to be a Member of the Grouping by giving not less than *(six) months' notice in writing to the other Members expiring *(on an Account Date) *(at any time) and on the expiry of such notice the cessation of Membership shall take effect.
6.2 Any Member shall immediately cease to be a Member of the Grouping if –
6.2.1 being an individual he dies;
6.2.2 he ceases to comply with the conditions laid down in Article 4(1) of the Regulation;
6.2.3 the law applicable to him, or the internal law of the State in which the Grouping has its official address, or a judicial or administrative decision made or recognised in a Member State requires that he shall cease to be a Member;
6.2.4 the other Members unanimously agree that he shall cease to be a Member. Written notice of such agreement shall be given to the outgoing Member;
6.2.5 he is expelled from Membership of the Grouping by the decision of a Court of competent jurisdiction.
6.3 The provisions of Schedule 4 shall apply on any cessation of membership.
6.4 Any outgoing Member shall continue to have obligations under this Agreement as set out in Schedule 5.

7. Transfer of Membership

7.1 Any Member may assign his participation in the Grouping, or a proportion thereof, either to another Member or to a third party but no such assignment shall take effect without the prior unanimous agreement of the other Members.
7.2 Any Member desirous of transferring his participation in the Grouping, or a proportion thereof shall give written notice to all the other Members not less than 14 clear days prior to the intended assignment. Such written notice shall state the identity of the intended new Member and any consideration to be paid for such an assignment.
7.3 The provisions of paragraphs 2.1, 2.2, 2.3 and 3 of Schedule 3 shall apply to any assignee of a Member's participation, but the remaining provisions of Schedule 3 shall not apply to such an assignee, unless otherwise unanimously agreed by the Members.

8. Use of Participation as Security

A Member may not use his participation in the Grouping as security in any form without the prior unanimous agreement of the other Members.

9. Rights and Obligations of Members

The Members shall have the rights and obligations set out in Schedule 6.

10. Liabilities of Members to Third Parties

10.1 The Members shall have unlimited joint and several liability for the debts of the Grouping of whatever nature.
10.2 Any Member who makes a payment of a debt of the Grouping of whatever nature shall be jointly and severally indemnified by the other Members and any outgoing Member (subject to the provisions of Schedule 4) to the extent that they are liable in accordance with Clause 4 and Schedule 2 of this Agreement.

11. Managers

11.1 Unless otherwise determined by unanimous agreement of the Members the number of Managers shall not be subject to any maximum but shall not be less than *(two).
11.2 The business of the Grouping shall be managed by the Managers who (subject to Clause 12 of this Agreement) may exercise all the powers of the Grouping not required by this Agreement to be exercised by the Members *(provided that the Grouping may only be bound by two or more Managers acting jointly).
11.3 The Managers may delegate any of their powers to any *(two Managers acting jointly) *(any individual Manager).
11.4 The first Managers of the Grouping shall be the persons named in Schedule 7, Part II. The Members may by unanimous agreement from time to time appoint additional Managers and remove Managers from office.
11.5 A Manager shall immediately cease to be a Manager if —

(i) he becomes prohibited by virtue of the law applicable to him or by virtue of the internal law of the State in which the Grouping has its official address or by virtue of a judicial or administrative decision made or recognised in a Member State from being a Manager;
(ii) he becomes mentally or physically incapable of acting as a Manager and is so certified as incapable by a medical practitioner approved by a majority of the Members;
(iii) he resigns his office by notice in writing to the Grouping;
(iv) all the Members *(a majority of the Members) *(unanimously) agree that he shall cease to be a Manager.

12. Restrictions on Powers of Managers

The Managers' powers shall be restricted in accordance with the provisions of Schedule 7, Part 1.

13. Duties of Managers

The Managers shall have the duties set out in Schedule 7, Part III.

14. Meetings of the Managers and Members and Notice

The calling of meetings of the Managers or Members and the holding and regulation of such meetings shall be in accordance with Schedule 8. The giving of any notice under the terms of this Agreement shall be in accordance with Part III of Schedule 8.

15. Members' Decisions

All decisions of the Members shall be taken by unanimous agreement save for those matters set out in Schedule 9.

The unanimous agreement of the Members shall either be given by each Member, or a duly authorised representative of a Member, voting in favour of a resolution at a meeting of the Members or by a resolution in writing signed or assented to by letter, telegram, telex, cable, facsimile or other written message by or on behalf of each Member which may consist of several documents in the like form each signed or purporting to have been despatched by or on behalf of one or more Members.

16. Minutes

16.1 A record of all proceedings of meetings of the Members and decisions of the Members under the terms of this Agreement and of all proceedings of meetings of the Managers and all resolutions in writing of the Managers shall be maintained in any form capable of being reproduced in legible form.
16.2 Any record of proceedings or decisions in legible form and purporting to be signed by *(two) Managers shall be prima facie evidence of such proceedings or decisions.

17. Accounts

17.1 The Managers shall cause accounting records to be properly written up and maintained for the Grouping and shall cause annual accounts comprising an income and expenditure account and a balance sheet and such other information, reports and accounts as they may deem appropriate or a majority of the Members may require to be prepared for presentation to the Members.
17.2 The annual accounts of the Grouping shall be prepared to the day of   in each year or to such other date as the Members may from time to time approve by unanimous agreement. A copy of the annual accounts shall be sent to every Member not more than *(seven) months after the date to which such accounts are prepared.

17.3 The currency of the Grouping for the drawing up of the annual accounts of the Grouping and calculating amounts apportioned, drawn, or due under this Agreement and for making payments and settling liabilities between Members and between Members and the Grouping shall be *(Pounds Sterling) or such other currency as the Members may unanimously agree.

17.4 The annual accounts shall be audited by Accountants appointed by a majority of the Members, or in default of such appointment, appointed by the Managers. Such Accountants may be removed from office at any time by resolution of a majority of the Members passed at a meeting of the Members and other Accountants may be appointed in their place. The Grouping Accountants appointed pursuant to this Clause shall prepare a report to the Members on the annual accounts of the Grouping which shall be sent to the Members with the annual accounts.

18. Currency Indemnity

18.1 Each Member hereby covenants with the Grouping and the other Members as obligations separate from and in addition to any other liability hereunder that:

18.1.1 it will indemnify the Grouping and the other Members against any loss, expense, liability or claim whatsoever in or arising from or incurred as a consequence of any default in payment of any sum payable by it hereunder or of any other breach by it of its obligations to it or them;

18.1.2 if any judgment or order given issued or entered by any court or tribunal for the payment of any sum to the Grouping by a Member or by one Member to another Member under or in relation to this Agreement (including without limiting the foregoing for the payment of damage in respect of any breach hereof) or other monies payable by one Member to another Member or by a Member to the Grouping hereunder is or are expressed in a currency other than *(Sterling) or being expressed in *(Sterling) is or are required for any purpose whatsoever to be converted into any other currency the relevant Member shall indemnify and hold harmless the other relevant Member and/or the Grouping from and against any loss to him arising or resulting from any difference between:

(i) the rate of exchange at which *(Sterling) is converted into such other currency for any such purpose as aforesaid; and

(ii) the rate of exchange at which he and/or the Grouping is able to purchase *(Sterling) with the amount of the other currency actually received by or into which the same is required to be converted by the Grouping or the other Member as appropriate.

Without limiting the foregoing 'the rate of exchange' includes any premiums and costs of exchange whatsoever payable in connection with the purchase of or conversion into or between currencies.

18.2 The indemnities constituted by the preceding sub-clause each constitute separate and independent obligations from each other obligation hereunder and shall have effect regardless of any indulgence of any kind granted by the Grouping or any Member and shall not be affected by any judgment being obtained or settlement effected in relation to any other obligation hereunder.
18.3 In enforcing the indemnity constituted by sub-clause **18.1** the Member or the Grouping shall not be required to give any proof or evidence of actual loss.

19. Dissolution

19.1 The Grouping must be wound up by decision of its Members or of the remaining Member if:

19.1.1 it no longer accords with Article 4(2) of the Regulation;

19.1.2 a majority of the Members pass a resolution at a meeting of the Members noting the accomplishment of the Grouping's purpose or the impossibility of pursuing it further.

19.2 Save as provided in Clause 19.1 above and in Schedule 4, a decision by the Members to wind up the Grouping may only be made by unanimous agreement of the Members after which any appropriate application may be made to a Court having competent jurisdiction.

20. Proper Law

This Agreement shall be governed by and subject to the laws of England.

21. Jurisdiction and Service

Each of the parties hereto hereby irrevocably submits to the non-exclusive jurisdiction of the courts of England and for the purposes of service of process hereby irrevocably appoints the person listed in Schedule 10 to accept service of process on his behalf.

22. Public Holidays

In the event that any matter required to be dealt with by this Agreement cannot be dealt with on the prescribed day due to a public holiday in any country it may be dealt with on the next day on which the banks would normally be open for business in that country.

Schedule 1

EEIG PARTICULARS

I NAME

II OFFICIAL ADDRESS

III OBJECTS

IV ORIGINAL MEMBERS

1. Name:

Business Name (if any):

Legal Form:

Permanent Address/Registered Office:

Registration Number (if any):

Place of Registration (if applicable):

2. Name:

Business Name (if any):

Legal Form:

Permanent Address/Registered Office:

Registration Number (if any):

Place of Registration (if applicable):

3. Name:

   Business Name (if any):

   Legal Form:

   Permanent Address/Registered Office:

   Registration Number (if any):

   Place of Registration (if applicable):

4. Name:

   Business Name (if any):

   Legal Form:

   Permanent Address/Registered Office:

   Registration Number (if any):

   Place of Registration (if applicable):

5. Name:

   Business Name (if any):

   Legal form:

   Permanent Address/Registered Office:

   Registration Number (if any):

   Place of Registration (if applicable):

V DURATION

Subject to the provisions for dissolution contained in this Agreement the Grouping shall continue for an indefinite duration.

Schedule 2

MEMBER	PROFITS	LOSSES	DISTRIBUTION OF ASSETS ON A WINDING UP

Schedule 3

ADMISSION OF NEW MEMBERS

1. If and whenever it is proposed to admit a New Member into the Grouping a meeting of the Members shall be convened to consider and decide by unanimous agreement:

1.1 whether to make an offer of Membership to the proposed New Member;

1.2 what shall be the Admission Date in relation to the proposed New Member;

1.3 what contribution or other provision of facilities (if any) the proposed New Member shall be required to make and what proportion of the profits and losses and assets on a winding up of the Grouping the proposed New Member shall be entitled to receive;

1.4 what adjustment to make in the respective contributions and proportionate shares of profits and losses and assets on a winding up of the Grouping of the existing Members in consequence of the admission of the proposed New Member;

1.5 whether the New Member is to be exempted from payment of debts and other liabilities of the Grouping which originated prior to the Admission Date of the New Member.

2. If it shall be decided to offer a Membership to the proposed New Member and if the proposed New Member shall accept such offer then:

2.1 the Proposed New Member shall be required by the Members to sign this Agreement in the space provided and in the presence of at least one existing Member or his authorised representative; and

2.2 a Minute shall be duly entered in the Minute Book and attached to this Agreement showing the names of the Members and their respective contributions and proportionate shares of the profits and losses and assets on a winding up of the Grouping consequent upon the admission of such Proposed New Member; and

2.3 appropriate details and forms shall be filed at all places where the Grouping is registered.

3. A person (not being an Original Member) shall not become a Member unless and until he has signed this Agreement as aforesaid and upon his signing this Agreement as aforesaid all the terms and provisions of this Agreement shall govern the relationship between that person and the other Members and between that person and the Grouping.

4. A New Member shall make such contribution (if any) as may be specified in the Minute referred to in sub-clause **2.2** above against the name of that New Member.

5. The respective contributions of the Members and their respective proportionate shares in the profits or losses or assets on a winding up of the

Grouping (adjusted as appropriate to take account of the admission of the New Member) shall be as specified in the said Minute subject to any alterations made thereafter by unanimous agreement.

Schedule 4

PROVISIONS APPLICABLE ON THE CESSATION OF MEMBERSHIP OF ANY MEMBER

Upon any Member becoming an Outgoing Member:

1. If the Continuing Members shall unanimously agree a Minute shall be duly entered in the Minute Book and attached to this Agreement showing the names of the Members and their respective contributions and proportionate shares of the profits and losses and assets on a winding up of the Grouping consequent upon the cessation of membership of that Member and appropriate details and forms shall be filed at all places where the Grouping is registered.
2. In default of unanimous agreement in accordance with paragraph 1 above as from the Succession Date the share of the Outgoing Member in the assets (including goodwill) of the Grouping and the entitlement of the Outgoing Member to participate in the profits of the Grouping and the requirement for the outgoing Member to bear the losses of the Grouping shall vest in the Continuing Members in proportion to their respective entitlements to share in the assets and profits and requirements to bear losses respectively immediately prior to the Succession Date.
3. The Continuing Members shall indemnify and keep indemnified the Outgoing Member and his estate or effects against (i) all debts and liabilities of the Grouping as at and after the Succession Date except any debt or liability in respect of tax attributable to the Outgoing Member's share of profits of the Grouping and except any debt or liability in respect of any claim arising from any wrongful act or omission of the Grouping or its Members or any of them to the extent that such claim is not covered by insurance and except any debt incurred by the Outgoing Member on behalf of the Grouping without the authority of the Managers and (ii) all actions, proceedings, costs, claims and demands in respect of such debts and liabilities except as aforesaid.

4.1 Any undrawn value of the Outgoing Member's share of the profits of the Grouping for the financial year of the Grouping in which the Succession Date occurs shall be paid to him as soon as the amount thereof has been ascertained by preparation and audit of the Annual Accounts for that financial year PROVIDED that unless a Succession Date occurs on an

Account Date such share shall be deemed to be a proportionate part calculated on a time basis of the share of the profits of the Grouping for that year to which the Outgoing Member would have been entitled if he had continued to be a Member for the whole of that year.

4.2 The Continuing Members shall pay to the Outgoing Member a capital sum equal to the value of the share of the Outgoing Member in the assets of the Grouping as at the Succession Date by not more than six equal instalments payable at six monthly intervals together with interest from the Succession Date on the amount from time to time outstanding of per centum per annum above the base rate for the time being of *(any leading Bank).

4.2.1 the first instalment to be payable at six months after the Succession Date or if later within seven days from the date upon which the amount of such capital sum shall have been agreed or determined in accordance with the provisions of this Agreement PROVIDED that if any such instalment shall be in arrear for more than 14 days the whole amount or balance of such capital sum then outstanding shall become immediately due and payable and shall bear interest thereafter to the date of payment at the rate of interest specified in the Clause above; and

4.2.2 the value of the share of the Outgoing Member in the assets of the Grouping at the Succession Date shall be agreed between the Outgoing Member and the Continuing Members and in default of such agreement within three months after the Succession Date shall be determined by the Grouping Accountants acting as experts whose decision shall be final and binding upon the parties affected by it and who in making such decision shall apply proper accountancy principles and may act upon such expert valuation advice as they think appropriate and so that the costs of such determination by the Grouping Accountants shall be borne as a revenue expense by the Grouping for the financial year in which the Succession Date occurs.

5. The liability of the Continuing Members to make the aforesaid payments and the liability under the indemnity or indemnities provided for herein shall be joint and several but as between themselves each such payment and any liability arising under such indemnity or indemnities shall be borne by them in the proportions in which the share in the assets of the Grouping of the Outgoing Member vested in them at the Succession Date.
6. If within a period of five weeks after the Succession Date a majority of the Members pass a resolution at a meeting of Members to wind up the Grouping, the Grouping shall be wound up and any appropriate application for the Grouping to be wound up may be made to a Court having competent jurisdiction and for the purposes of the winding up the Outgoing Member shall be deemed to be a Member and the foregoing provisions 1 to 5 (inclusive) of this Schedule shall not apply.

Schedule 5

CONTINUING OBLIGATIONS OF AN OUTGOING MEMBER

After his cessation of membership an Outgoing Member:

1. shall forthwith deliver to the Grouping all property of the Grouping and all papers deeds and documents in his possession or under his control and relating to the affairs of the Grouping or relating to the affairs of a Member which he has obtained through his membership of the Grouping;
2. shall forthwith pay to the Grouping any sums owing from that Outgoing Member to the Grouping or to any other Member under the terms of this Agreement on the Succession Date or shall pay as soon thereafter as the same shall be ascertained and in default of such payment the balance of such sum outstanding shall bear interest thereafter to the date of payment at the rate of per centum per annum above the base rate for the time being of *(any leading bank);
3. shall not represent himself or permit himself to be represented as acting on behalf of the Grouping or being connected with or a successor to the Grouping;
4. shall not represent, promote, advertise or refer to his previous connection with the Grouping in such a way as to utilise any goodwill or trading reputation of the Grouping;
5. shall not carry on, cause or permit any business to be carried on under or using any name style, logo or image which the Grouping may have used or which includes all or any material part of any such name, style, logo or image or which is a name style, logo or image in the opinion of the majority of the Continuing Members calculated to cause confusion between the one so used by the Grouping and the one in question or to give rise to an inference or connection with the Grouping;
6. shall not at any time before the expiration of six months from the Succession Date seek to entice away from the Grouping or solicit the employment or engagement in office or membership in another EEIG or any other legal entity any other person who at the time of or at any time during the six months preceding the Succession Date was a Member, Manager or employee of the Grouping or an employee of another Member;
7. shall not within *(12 months) after the Succession Date use his knowledge of the business requirements of or exert any influence over or canvass or by any other means seek or solicit business or orders from all or any person or persons who or which at any time during the period of *(one year) before the Succession Date was a client or customer or prospective client or customer of the Grouping other than a client or customer of the Grouping introduced to the Grouping by the Outgoing Member with a view to obtaining orders

for any goods or services of a type supplied or rendered by the Grouping during the *(one year) preceding cessation.

Schedule 6

RIGHTS AND OBLIGATIONS OF MEMBERS

1. Each Member shall have the following rights:

1.1 At any time upon giving reasonable notice either himself or through his representatives or agents to inspect and take copies of and require information regarding the accounting records and Minutes of the Grouping.

1.2 To requisition a meeting of the Members by giving 21 days' notice in writing to the other Members stating the objects of the Meeting.

1.3 To require that any Manager shall be present at any meeting of the Members.

1.4 To be given notice of every meeting of the Members and to attend and vote at and otherwise participate in such a meeting.

2. Each Member shall have the following obligations and each Member undertakes:

2.1 to observe the provisions of this Agreement and any amendments thereto;

2.2 to provide funding and facilities for the Grouping in accordance with the terms of this Agreement;

2.3 at all times not to disclose and to use all reasonable endeavours to ensure that its officers, employees and agents do not disclose any Confidential Information which it may acquire in relation to the Grouping or in relation to any other Member through the affairs of the Grouping except with the consent of the Grouping or the other Member as the case may be or for the proper purposes of the Grouping or in accordance with the order of a court of competent jurisdiction;

2.4 to provide the Grouping Accountants with all information which they may reasonably require to prepare the accounts of the Grouping;

2.5 at all times not to use or attempt to use the name or goodwill of the Grouping save in connection with the proper purposes of the Grouping;

2.6 whilst he is a Member not to directly or indirectly be engaged, concerned or interested in any other EEIG which competes with the objects or businesses of the Grouping;

2.7 to declare fully to the Grouping by notice in writing any interest which he may have in a proposed contract or existing contract with the Grouping either prior to the Grouping entering into such contract or forthwith upon him becoming so interested as the case may be.

Schedule 7

PART I

RESTRICTIONS ON THE POWERS OF MANAGERS

None

PART II

Manager	*Address*
1.	
2.	
3.	

PART III

It is the duty of each Manager:

1. who is in any way, whether directly or indirectly, interested in a contract or proposed contract with the Grouping to declare the nature of his interest at a meeting of the Managers either at the meeting of the Managers at which the question of entering into the contract is first taken into consideration or if the Manager is not at the date of that meeting interested in the proposed contract, at the next meeting of the Managers held after he became so interested in the proposed contract or existing contract; and
2. to avoid entering into any relations with third parties which will involve him in any conflict of interest with his position as Manager save with the prior consent of a majority of the Members of the Grouping; and
3. not to make any profit from his position as Manager apart from that provided for in any contract with the Grouping save with the prior consent of a majority of the Members of the Grouping and to account to the Grouping for any profit made by him in contravention of this provision; and
4. to give to the Members details of the Grouping's accounts, assets, liabilities, budgets and other affairs as they may reasonably require; and
5. to satisfy the requirements of the Regulation and any national legislation made by a member state thereunder with regard to the filing of information regarding the Grouping at any time after its registration.

Schedule 8

PART I

MEETINGS OF THE MANAGERS

1. The Managers shall meet not less than *(four) times in each calendar year.
2. Any Manager may call a meeting of the Managers by not less than seven clear days' notice in writing sent to every Manager by post, telex or facsimile machine provided that a meeting may be called by shorter notice if every Manager so agrees in writing by letter, telex, facsimile transmission or any other form of written communication. The accidental non-receipt of notice of a meeting by any person entitled to receive notice shall not invalidate proceedings at that meeting.
3. The quorum for meetings of the Managers shall be fixed by the Managers and unless so fixed at any other number shall be two.
4. Questions arising at a meeting of the Managers shall be decided by a majority of votes and each Manager shall have one vote. In the case of an equality of votes a resolution shall be deemed not passed. The Managers may otherwise regulate the conduct of their meetings as they think fit.
5. A resolution in writing signed or assented to by letter, telegram, telex, cable, facsimile or other written message by all the Managers shall be as valid and effectual as if it had been passed at a meeting of the Managers and may consist of several documents in the like form each signed or purporting to have been despatched by one or more Managers.

PART II

MEETINGS OF THE MEMBERS

1. The Members shall meet not less than *(once) in each calendar year.
2. Any Member and any two Managers acting jointly may call a meeting of the Members by not less than 21 clear days' notice in writing sent to every Member provided that a meeting may be called by shorter notice if every Member so agrees in writing by letter, telex, facsimile transmission or any other form of written communication. The accidental non-receipt of a notice of a meeting by any person entitled to receive notice shall not invalidate proceedings at that meeting.
3. The quorum for meetings of the Members shall be *(all) *(three of) the Members present in person or by their duly authorised representative at any meeting of the Members and he may exercise on behalf of his appointing Member the same powers as the Member could exercise at that meeting.
4. Save as provided in Clause 15 of this Agreement and this Schedule the Members may regulate the conduct of their meetings as they think fit.

PART III

1. Any notice required to be sent to a Manager or Member in accordance with this agreement shall be sent to such address, telex number or facsimile number as he shall have provided to the Grouping for such service.
2. 'Clear days' in relation to the period of a notice means in relation to each Manager or Member receiving such notice that period excluding any day on which the banks in the country of the recipient would not normally be open for business and excluding the day on which the notice is given or deemed given and excluding the day for which it is given or on which it is to take effect.
3. Notice sent by telex or facsimile shall be deemed to be given one hour after transmission and notice sent by post shall be deemed to be given 72 hours after prepaid posting.

Schedule 9

NONE

Schedule 10

MEMBER	PERSON AND ADDRESS FOR SERVICE

Schedule 11

INTERPRETATION

'Account date'	– means the date to which an income and expenditure account and balance sheet shall be prepared in accordance with Clause 17.2 of this Agreement
'Admission Date'	– means in relation to a New Member the date of his admission as a New Member
'this Agreement'	– means the Agreement to which this is a Schedule and includes the *(11) Schedules
'Annual Accounts'	– means the accounts, information and reports prepared in accordance with Clause 17.1 of this Agreement
'Clear Days'	– means a number of days calculated in accordance with the provisions of Part III of Schedule 8 of this Agreement

'Confidential Information'	– means any and all information of a secret or confidential nature which relates to or is used in the business of the Grouping or of a Member or in which the Grouping or a Member otherwise has an interest and which has not for the time being manifestly and demonstrably come into the public domain including (without limitation): (i) know-how technical information expertise designs data formulae processes specifications and other intellectual knowledge and information; (ii) drawings writings and other papers computer programs and other tangible and non-tangible manifestations of any items referred to in paragraph (i) of this definition; (iii) all rights to and copyright patent registered design trade marks and other protection for or relating to the foregoing; (iv) customer supplier and price lists marketing plans terms of contracts agreements or arrangements and business information generally; (v) organisational management personnel and administrative information generally; and (vi) any matters of a like nature which is confidential information by virtue of its nature and can be shown to be reasonably likely to result in damage or loss to the Grouping or a Member if disclosed to competitors or other unauthorised persons;
'Continuing Members'	– means the Members of the Grouping immediately prior to a Succession Date other than the Outgoing Member who ceases to be a Member on that Succession Date
'Grouping'	– means the European Economic Interest Grouping registered pursuant to this Agreement
'Grouping Accountants'	– means the Accountants appointed by the Members to audit the annual accounts in

	accordance with Clause **17.4** of this Agreement
'Member'	– means any Original Member and any New Member provided that he has not become an Outgoing Member
'Minute Book'	– means the record of proceedings of meetings and decisions maintained in accordance with Clause **16** of this Agreement
'New Member'	– means any natural person company firm or other legal body who shall subsequent to the execution of this Agreement be admitted to membership of the Grouping in accordance with Clause 5 and Schedule 3 of this Agreement
'Outgoing Member'	– means any natural person company firm or other legal body who ceases to be a Member either in accordance with the provisions of Clause 6 of this Agreement or under any other provision of law
'Registration'	– means the giving of a Certificate by the Registrar that the Grouping has been registered
'Regulation'	– means Council Regulation (EEC) No 2137/85 of 25 July 1985 on the European Economic Interest Grouping (EEIG)
'Succession Date'	- means in relation to an Outgoing Member the date of his becoming an Outgoing Member

References to the masculine include the feminine and neuter and references to person include company firm or other legal body and references to the singular include the plural and vice versa.

The headings in this Agreement are for ease of reference only and shall not in any way affect the construction of this Agreement.

References to any statute, statutory provision or the Regulation include references to any amendment, re-enactment or replacement of the same for the time being in force.

Unless the context otherwise requires, words or expressions used in this Agreement shall bear the same meaning as in the Regulation or any modification thereof in force.

Original Members

Signed by

for and on behalf of

in the presence of:

Signed by

for and on behalf of

in the presence of:

Signed by

for and on behalf of

in the presence of:

Signed by

for and on behalf of

in the presence of:

New Members

Signed by

for and on behalf of

in the presence of:

Signed by

for and on behalf of

in the presence of:

Signed by

for and on behalf of

in the presence of:

Notes to Clauses

PREAMBLE

This may be changed or added to as necessary.

1. **Interpretation**

   This has been inserted in a Schedule so that additions may more easily be inserted if there are additional clauses in the Agreement which require interpretation.

2. **Preconditions**

   Additional preconditions may be inserted. In such a case it may be appropriate to insert provisions to allow breach of preconditions to be waived. A Schedule detailing charges which constitute a charge over participation in or membership of the Grouping should be added if required.

   Warranties

   It may be desired to insert warranties into the Agreement, which if breached may either give entitlement to damages or to terminate the Agreement.

3. **Agreement to Form the Grouping**

   The items in Clause **3.1** and Schedule 1 are compulsory. All details should be completed. The name of the Grouping must end in the words 'European Economic Interest Grouping' or the initials 'EEIG'.

   Insert the name of the party responsible for registration.

   Provision has been made with regard to costs of the Agreement and registration.

4. **Funding and Division of Profits and Losses**

   Clause **4.1** contains alternatives which should be deleted or altered as required. Either the budget or the Schedule should contain agreed valuations of the assets which the Members contribute to the Grouping. It may also be appropriate to arrange for regular valuations.

   Professional advice must be sought with regard to the taxation consequences of the different methods of funding the Grouping.

   More specific provision may be inserted in Clause **4.5**.

   In Clause **4.6** the percentage rate may be by reference to any required standard.

   Schedule 2 may be drawn as required. Professional advice should be sought regarding the taxation consequences, particularly with regard to the asset sharing ratio.

5. **Admission of New Members**

   The provisions of Schedule 3 may be redrawn if required.

6. **Cessation of Membership**

   Clause **6.1** makes provision for voluntary cessation of membership. It contains alternatives. Other provisions may be required if appropriate.

   Clause **6.2** makes provision for compulsory cessation of membership.

Alterations or additions to Clause 6 may be made as required.

Schedule 4 makes various provisions for altering the participation of the Members, paying the Outgoing Member for his share in the Grouping and provides an alternative that a majority of the Members may resolve within five weeks of a Member leaving that the Grouping be wound up. Different provisions may be inserted if desired.

Schedule 5 makes provision regarding the continuing obligations of an Outgoing Member. Further or other restrictive covenants may be required.

7. **Transfer of Membership**

Article 22 of the Regulation provides that a Member may only assign his participation with the unanimous authorisation of the other Members.

8. **Use of Participation as Security**

Article 22 of the Regulation provides that a Member may use his participation as security only after the other Members have given their unanimous authorisation unless otherwise provided in the formation contract. This clause prohibits use of participation as security without the prior unanimous agreement of the other Members.

9. **Rights and Obligations of Members**

These may be altered or extended as required. Services which the Members must provide to the Grouping and other such matters might be inserted. 'Confidential Information' is defined in Schedule 11.

10. **Liabilities of Members to Third Parties**

This re-states the unlimited liability of the Members and provides for indemnity.

11. **Managers**

Clause **11.1** sets out the maximum and minimum number of Managers.

Clause **11.2** contains an option to provide that the Grouping may only be bound by two or more Managers acting jointly, if not included, any single Manager may bind the Grouping. If Managers are required to act jointly, letters, order forms and similar documents of the Grouping must indicate this.

Clause **11.3** provides alternatives for delegation of powers.

Clause **11.4** and Schedule 7 name the first Managers. Provision is made for additional Managers to be appointed by unanimous agreement of the Members. An alternative provision might be made for each Member to have the right to appoint and remove one or more Managers.

12. **Restrictions on the Powers of Managers**

If any restrictions are to be entered, these will be ineffective against Third Parties. However it may be useful for the Members to reach agreement amongst themselves about such restrictions. Similarly, it may be useful to set out agreed duties of Managers as, for example in Schedule 7, Part III. It is recommended that the Managers have service contracts.

13. **Duties of Managers**

See note 12.

14. Meetings of Managers and Members
Schedule 8 should be altered as required. For instance more detailed provisions regarding a Chairman, proxies or adjournment of meetings may be required. Provision might be inserted to hold meetings by telephone, etc.

15. Members' Decisions
Schedule 9 has been left blank, as suitable contents are likely to alter with the circumstances of different EEIGs.

16. Minutes
This provides a method of recording and providing proof of decisions.

17. Accounts
Please note the date to which accounts are made up, the currency and the time within which they should be presented to the Members should be inserted. More detailed provisions regarding the accounts and the Accountants' Report can be inserted if required.

18. Currency Indemnity

19. Dissolution
It may be appropriate to provide in Clause **19.2** for dissolution by a majority if appropriate.

20. Proper Law
This Agreement will be subject to the laws of England.

21. Jurisdiction and Service
A clause of this type may simplify service.

22. Public Holidays
This recognises that the Agreement will operate between various persons enjoying different public holidays.

CHECK-LIST OF CLAUSES IN AN EEIG AGREEMENT

	Required by Regulation	Sample Clause in Jordans Example of Agreement	May be appropriate
PREAMBLE		✓	
PARTIES		Sch 1	
INTERPRETATION		1	
PRECONDITIONS TO THE AGREEMENT		2	
WARRANTIES		2	
AGREEMENT TO FORM THE EEIG	✓	3.1, Sch 1	
(i) Name	✓	Sch 1	
(ii) Official Address	✓	Sch 1	
(iii) Objects	✓	Sch 1	
(iv) Name, business name, legal form, permanent address or registered office, and number and place of registration, if any, of each Member	✓	Sch 1	
(v) Duration (except where indefinite)	✓	Sch 1	
(vi) Responsibility to Register		3.3	
(vii) Formation expenses		3.2, 3.4	
(viii) PAYE Registration			✓
(ix) Members' Tax Liability			✓
(x) Members' Pension and Insurance Liabilities and Entitlement			✓

	Required by Regulation	Sample Clause in Jordans Example of Agreement	May be appropriate
FUNDING AND DIVISION OF PROFIT AND LOSSES			
(i) Capital and other contributions and funding		**4.1**	
(ii) Profit		**4.2, Sch 2**	
(iii) Losses		**4.2, Sch 2**	
(iv) Distribution on a winding up		**4.2, Sch 2**	
(v) Drawings		**4.5, 4.6**	
(vi) Incapacity of Members			✓
(vii) Alteration of Participation			✓
ASSETS OF THE GROUPING			✓
(i) Goodwill			✓
ADMISSION OF NEW MEMBERS			✓
(i) Decision to admit and conditions of admission		**5, Sch 3**	
(ii) Warranty of New Member			✓
MEMBERS VOLUNTARILY LEAVING		**6.1, Sch 4**	
COMPULSORY CESSATION OF MEMBERSHIP		**6.2, Sch 4**	
(i) Grounds of mandatory expulsion		**6.2**	✓
(ii) Grounds for discretionary expulsion			✓
(iii) Other consequences of acts entitling expulsion			✓

	Required by Regulation	Sample Clause in Jordans Example of Agreement	May be appropriate
EFFECTS OF CESSATION OF MEMBERSHIP		**6.3, Sch 4**	
(i) Adjustment of rights and liabilities		**Sch 4**	
(ii) Option to decide to wind up		**Sch 4**	
(iii) Effect of cessation (eg on other agreements)			✓
(iv) Indemnity of Outgoing Member			✓
(v) Taxation, Insurance, VAT			✓
CONTINUING OBLIGATIONS OF AN OUTGOING MEMBER		**6.4, Sch 5**	
(i) Restrictive covenants		**Sch 5**	
(ii) Liability of Outgoing Members for past liabilities		**Sch 4**	✓
(iii) Indemnity			✓
TRANSFER OF MEMBERSHIP		**7**	
(i) Notice of intended transfer		**7.1**	
(ii) Pre-emption on transfer			✓
(iii) Form of transfer			✓
(iv) Registration of transfer			✓
USE OF PARTICIPATION AS SECURITY		**8**	
(i) Use			✓
(ii) Type of security			✓

	Required by Regulation	Sample Clause in Jordans Example of Agreement	May be appropriate
RIGHTS OF MEMBERS		Sch 6	
(i) To have notice of, attend and vote at meetings		Sch 6	
(ii) To requisition meetings of the Members		Sch 6	
(iii) Financial information		Sch 6	
(iv) Obtain Grouping's Services			✓
(v) Hold assets on trust			✓
(vi) Re-imbursement of expenses			✓
(vii) Pre-emption on transfer			✓
(viii) Elect Members to Committees (eg study of performance programmes)			✓
OBLIGATIONS OF MEMBERS		Sch 6	
(i) Devotion of time and resources			✓
(ii) Observe Agreement		Sch 6	
(iii) Comply with requests of Grouping			✓
(iv) Provide information for Accounts		Sch 6	
(v) Non-competitive covenant		Sch 6	
(vi) Further covenants			✓
(vii) Disclosure of interests		Sch 6	
(viii) Use of the Groupings assets			✓
(ix) Signing of cheques			✓

	Required by Regulation	Sample Clause in Jordans Example of Agreement	May be appropriate
LIABILITY OF MEMBERS TO THIRD PARTIES		10	
(i) Joint and several liability		10.1	
(ii) Payments to Third Parties			✓
(iii) Indemnity		10.2	
(iv) Accounting to the Grouping for Grouping benefits			✓
MANAGERS		11, Sch 7	
(i) Number		11.1	
(ii) Management powers and whether bound only by two or more Managers acting jointly		11.2	
(iii) Persons who may be Managers			✓
(iv) Delegation of Managers' powers		11.3	
DUTIES OF MANAGERS		13, Sch 7	✓
RIGHTS OF MANAGERS			✓
RESTRICTIONS ON POWERS OF MANAGERS (NB These are ineffective against Third Parties)		12, Sch 7	
APPOINTMENT OF MANAGERS		11.4	
RETIREMENT OF MANAGERS			✓
CHAIRMAN			✓
MEETINGS OF MANAGERS		14, Sch 8	

	Required by Regulation	Sample Clause in Jordans Example of Agreement	May be appropriate
MEETINGS OF MEMBERS		**14, Sch 8**	
MEMBERS' DECISIONS		**15, Sch 9**	
(i) Matters requiring unanimity/majority		**15, Sch 9**	
MINUTES		**16**	
ACCOUNTING MATTERS		**17**	
(i) Format and responsibility for preparation		**17.1**	
(ii) Accounting date		**17.2**	
(iii) Currency		**17.3**	
(iv) Audit		**17.4**	
(v) Presentation/despatch to Members		**17.2, 17.4**	
CURRENCY INDEMNITY		**18**	
WINDING UP		**19**	
(i) Unanimous/majority decision		**19.2**	
PROPER LAW		**20**	
JURISDICTION AND SERVICE		**21**	
PUBLIC HOLIDAYS		**22**	
METHODS OF DISPUTE RESOLUTION			✓

APPENDIX II

Registration Formalities for Member States

BELGIUM

EEIG Formation

1. NAME: Europees Economisch Samenwerkingsverband/Groupement Européen d'Intérêt Economique.
2. ACRONYM: EESV/GEIE.
3. NAME OF LAW: Wet san 12 juli 1989 houdende verscheidene maatregelen tot toepassing van de Verordening (EEG) nr 2137/85 van de Raad van 25 juli 1985 tot instelling van Europese economische samenwerkingsverbanden/Loi du 12 juillet 1989 portant diverses mesures d'application du Réglement (CEE) No 2137/85 du Conseil du 25 juillet 1985 relatif à l'institution d'un groupement européen d'intérêt économique. A Royal Decree providing rules on registration and publication requirements was issued on 27 July 1989.
4. COMMENCEMENT DATE: 22 August 1989.

EEIGs with Commercial Objects

5. DESIGNATED REGISTRY— **address**
   1. At the Handelsregister/Registre de Commerce (commercial registry) of the local Rechtbank van Koophandel/Tribunal de Commerce (commercial bank) having jurisdiction where the EEIG will have its official address.
   2. Reference address for information: Rechtbank van Koophandel/Tribunal de Commerce Rue Paul Devauxstraat 5
      B-1000 Brussel/Bruxelles.

      Tel: 32 2512 7448 or 32 2512 7512
6. DOCUMENTS TO BE FILED: Formation Agreement, executed by notarial deed or by private deed, in the language of the part of the country where the EEIG has its official address. Belgium has four language regions: Dutch speaking, German speaking, French speaking and Brussels (French or Dutch may be used). Any powers of attorney relied upon at execution must also be filed.
7. FORMS: Formule I (French) or Formulier 1 (Dutch) for the registration of commercial EEIGs.

8. PROCEDURE: Agreement and Form to be filed within 15 days of execution of agreement.

9. REGISTRATION FEES: BF 2,400 per page.

10. EVIDENCE OF REGISTRATION: Within 15 days after filing, registration details are published in the Belgusch Staatsblad/Moniteur Belge. Details must be sent for publication in the Official Journal of the European Communities within one month of publication in the Belgian Official Gazette.

EEIGs with Non-Commercial Objects

If the objects laid down in the formation contract do not include commercial acts in the sense of Arts 2 and 3 of the Belgian Commercial Code, no registration is necessary.

DENMARK

EEIG Formation

1. NAME: Europæiske økonomiske firmagrupper.
2. ACRONYM: EØFG.
3. NAME OF LAW: Lov nr. 217 af 5 april 1989 om administration af Det Europæiske Økonomiske Fællesskabs forordninger om indførelse af europæiske økonomiske firmagrupper; Administrative Rules, Nos 534 and 535 were issued on 7 August 1989.
4. COMMENCEMENT DATE: 5 April 1989.
5. DESIGNATED REGISTRY—**address**
   Registrar of Companies
   in Copenhagen:
   Erhvervs- eg Selskabsstyrelsen,
   Kampmannsgade 1,
   DK-Copenhagen, 1604 V
   Denmark.

   Tel: 33 124280
   Fax: 33 324480
6. DOCUMENTS TO BE FILED: Formation Agreement.
7. FORMS: Anmeldelse til Erhvervs- eg Selskabsstyrelsen register for europæiske økonomiske firmagrupper.
8. PROCEDURE: Formation Agreement and forms to be filed within four weeks of execution of Agreement.
9. REGISTRATION FEES: Dkr 1700.
10. EVIDENCE OF REGISTRATION: Registration number and certificate are issued. Notice of registration is published in the Statstidende and the Official Journal of the European Communities (EF-Tidende).

EIRE

EEIG Formation

1. NAME: European Economic Interest Grouping (Grupail Eorpach um Leas Eacnamaioch).
2. ACRONYM: EEIG (GELE).
3. NAME OF LAW: European Communities (European Economic Interest Groupings) Regulations 1989 (SI 1989/191) ('Regulations').
4. COMMENCEMENT DATE: 1 August 1989.
5. DESIGNATED REGISTRY—**address**
   Companies Registration Office
   Lower Castle Yard
   Dublin Castle
   Dublin 2
   Ireland.

   Tel: 353 1614222
   Tlx: 91365
6. DOCUMENTS TO BE FILED: Formation Agreement.
7. FORMS (set out in the second Schedule of the Regulations): IG1; IG5.
8. PROCEDURE: Formation Agreement and forms IG1 and IG5 to be filed within 14 days of execution.
9. REGISTRATION FEES: IR£150.
10. EVIDENCE OF REGISTRATION: Registrar issues a Certificate of Registration.

The EEIG must publish certain particulars as set out in the Regulations in the Irish Oifigiuil within 21 days of registration. Publication in the Official Journal of the European Communities is carried out by the Registrar.

FRANCE

EEIG Formation

1. NAME: Groupement Européen d'Intérêt Économique.
2. ACRONYM: GEIE.
3. NAME OF LAW: La loi 89/377 du 13 juin 1989; Royal Decree of 20 June 1989 provides rules for registering EEIGs.
4. COMMENCEMENT DATE: 13 juin 1989.
5. DESIGNATED REGISTRY—reference addresses for information.

   example 1
   Where the EEIG has its official address, at the Registre de Commerce et des Sociétés (Register of Commerce and Companies) which is a department of the local Tribunal de Commerce (Commercial Court). There is at least one for each of the 95 administrative Departements in France.
   Le Centre des Formalités d' Entreprises ('CFE')
   Chambre de Commerce de l'Ile-de-France
   1 Quai de Corse
   F-75004 Paris, France.

   Tel: 33 1 43 29 12 60

   example 2
   M le Greffier
   Chambre de Commerce et d'Industrie de Lyon
   20 rue de la Bourse
   69289 Lyon Cedex 02.

   Tel: 33 72 40 58 58
   Fax: 33 78 37 53 46
   Tlx: 310828

6. DOCUMENTS TO BE FILED (a complete list can be obtained from CFE): Two copies or originals of the Formation Agreement. Two copies of any separate document naming the Managers (unless included in the Formation Agreement). Birth certificates of the Manager(s) and financial controller(s). The K-bis statements of Members which are French corporate bodies. Certified copies of the bye-laws of foreign corporate bodies.

The marriage contracts and other personal information of Members who are private individuals, both French and foreign.

7. FORMS: Form C1, request for registration in triplicate Declaration de Constitution de Société en autre Personne Morale relevant du RCS.

8. PROCEDURE: Once the documents have been filed with the CFE, they will be transmitted to all the necessary government agencies and organisations, and in particular, the Tribunal de Commerce. This involves a delay of three to four days.

9. REGISTRATION FEES: Ff 1,190.77. If there is capital (or assets) in the EEIG, a set tax of 1 per cent of the capital (or assets) is payable.

10. EVIDENCE OF REGISTRATION: Initial publication in local gazette followed by advertisement in the Official Bulletin of civil and commercial notices (BODACC) and in the Official Journal of the European Communities. Statement of compliance is issued by registrar on registration.

11. Once the documents have been filed with the CFE, they will be transmitted to all the necessary government agencies and organisations, and in particular, the Tribunal de Commerce. This involves a delay of three to four days.

GREAT BRITAIN & NORTHERN IRELAND

EEIG Formation

1. NAME: European Economic Interest Grouping.
2. ACRONYM: EEIG.
3. NAME OF LAW: United Kingdom European Economic Interest Grouping Regulations 1989 (SI 1989/638).
   European Economic Interest Grouping Regulations (Northern Ireland) 1989.
4. COMMENCEMENT DATE: UK Regulations: 1 July 1989
   Northern Ireland Regulations: 17 July 1989.
5. DESIGNATED REGISTRY— address

England & Wales	*Scotland*
Companies House	Companies House
Crown Way	102 George St
Maindy	Edinburgh
Cardiff	EH2 3DJ.
South Glamorgan	
CF4 3UZ.	
Tel: 44 222 380529	44 31 225 5774
Fax: each dept has own number	44 31 220 4820
Tlx: 497768	

address

Northern Ireland
Companies House
IDB House
64 Chichester St
Belfast BT1 4JX.

Tel: 44 232 234488
Fax: 44 232 231328

6. DOCUMENTS TO BE FILED: Formation Agreement.
7. FORMS (set out in Schedule 2 of each of the Regulations): EEIG 1. Formation Agreement and form EEIG 1 to be delivered within 15 days of execution of Agreement.
8. PROCEDURE: Agreements not in English to be accompanied by a certified translation.
9. REGISTRATION FEES: £50.
10. EVIDENCE OF REGISTRATION: Registrar issues certificate of registration being conclusive evidence that the requirements of the Regulation and Statutory Instrument have been complied with. He then publishes an advertisement in the London, Edinburgh or Belfast Gazette and the Official Journal of the European Communities.

GREECE

Greece is amending its Commercial Code and will include provisions for registration of EEIGs in its revised code.

ITALY

EEIG Formation

1. NAME: Gruppo Europeo di Interesse Economico.
2. ACRONYM: GEIE.
3. NAME OF LAW: Bill introduced before Italian Government in April 1989.
4. COMMENCEMENT DATE: N/A
5. DESIGNATED REGISTRY—**address**
   It is anticipated registration will initially take place at the Cancelleria office of the local civil court.

   When the registry for enterprises is set up, registration will take place there.

   Tel: N/A
   Fax: N/A
   Tlx: N/A
6. DOCUMENTS TO BE FILED: Formation Agreement and details required by Arts 6, 7 and 10 of the EC Regulation.
7. FORMS: N/A
8. PROCEDURE: Formation Agreement to be presented to the local registry within 30 days of execution.
9. REGISTRATION FEES: N/A
10. EVIDENCE OF REGISTRATION:
    Publication in the Gazzetta Ufficiale of the Italian Republic and the Official Journal of the European Communities within 30 days from registration.

LUXEMBOURG

EEIG Formation

1. NAME: Groupement Européen d' Intérêt Économique.
2. ACRONYM: GEIE.
3. NAME OF LAW: No registration procedure has been implemented, nor is any draft law available in Luxembourg at the time of writing.

NETHERLANDS

EEIG Formation

1. NAME: Europees Economisch Samenwerkingsverband.
2. ACRONYM: EESV.
3. NAME OF LAW: Wet van 28 juni 1989 houdende uitvoering van de Verordening nr 2137/85 van de Raad van de Europese Gemeenschappen van 25 juli 1985 tot instelling van Europese economische samenwerkingsverbanden.
4. COMMENCEMENT DATE: 1 July 1989.
5. DESIGNATED REGISTRY—**address**
   The commercial registry at the chamber of commerce in the canton in which the EEIG has its official address, eg:

   Handelsregister van de Kamer van
   Koophandel en Fabrieken te Amsterdam (Commercial Registry)
   Koningin Wilhelminaplein 13
   NL-1062 HH Amsterdam.

   Tel: 31 20 172882
   Fax: 31 20 172493
   Tlx: 18888
6. DOCUMENTS TO BE FILED: Original or authenticated Formation Agreement. Certain additional information with regard to any enterprise which is affiliated with the EEIG and the managers of the EEIG.
7. FORMS: Available on request.
8. PROCEDURE: Documents accepted in Dutch, English, French and German. Otherwise a translation into Dutch is required. EEIG has legal personality from the date of registration. If the Formation Agreement has not been laid down in the form of a notarial deed, a copy of the Contract must be authenticated by all the Members.
9. REGISTRATION FEES: On a scale dependent on the capital of the EEIG.
10. EVIDENCE OF REGISTRATION: Details of the EEIG must be published in the Dutch Government Gazette De Nederlandse Staatscourant and the Official Journal of the European Communities.

PORTUGAL

EEIG Formation

1. NAME: Agrupamento Europeu de Interesse Economico.
2. ACRONYM: AEIE.
3. NAME OF LAW: Decree-Law 148/90 of 9 May 1990 containing the main rules implementing the Regulation, by force of which, in matters not covered by said Regulation and Decree-Law 4/73 of 4 June 1973 and Decree-Law 430/73 of 25 August 1973 governing Agrupamentos Complementares de Empresas (Ancillary Company Groupings) shall also apply in the implementation of the Regulation: Codigo de Registe Comercial (Commercial Registry Code) adopted under Decree-Law 403/86 of 3 December 1986 on matters relating to registration, and Codigo de Imposte sobre Rendimento das Pessoas Colectivas (Company Income Tax Code) adopted under Decree-Law 443-B/88 of 30 November 1988, on tax aspects.
4. COMMENCEMENT DATE: Decree-Law 148/90 came into force on 8 June 1990.
5. DESIGNATED REGISTRY—**address**
   Registration takes place at the local commercial registry, Conservatoria do Registro Comercial in the area in which the EGIG's official address is situated. Two examples are:

   example 1
   Conservatoria do Registo Comercial
   Rua Nova do Almada 35
   1200 Lisboa
   Portugal.

   Tel: 351 3461556

   example 2
   eg Conservatoria do Registo Comercial
   Rua de Canta, 16-2e andar
   4000 Porto
   Portugal.

   Tel: 351-21742
6. DOCUMENTS TO BE FILED: Formation Agreement to be filed within 90 days of execution.

7. FORMS: Forms to be filed are obtainable from the respective authorities, ie Conservatorias de Registo Comercial, ICEP (Institute of Portuguese Foreign Trade) and Registo Nacional de Pessoas Colectivas.

8. PROCEDURE: Certificate of authorisation of the name must be obtained in advance of registration from the Registo Nacional de Pessoas Colectivas. Any documents not in Portuguese must be translated and notarised. If any Member of the EEIG is a non-resident, filing with the ICEP (Institute of Portuguese Foreign Trade) is also necessary.

9. REGISTRATION FEES: Name authorisation: PTE 4000–PTE 19000 depending on whether it is Portuguese or not.

   Registration at commercial registry—PTE 3000 plus variable capital duty.

   Registration at Registo Nacional de Pessoas Colectivas: PTE 1000 plus 0.5 per cent of capital or 1 per cent capital for foreign name.

10. EVIDENCE OF REGISTRATION: Local commercial registrar publishes Formation Agreement in the Diario de Republica (the national official gazette) and registration of the EEIG at the Registo Nacional de Pessoas Colectivas. Notice of registration is published in the Official Journal of the European Communities.

SPAIN

EEIG Formation

1. NAME: Agrupación Europea de Interés Económico.
2. ACRONYM: AEIE.
3. NAME OF LAW: Articles 228 to 233 of the new Regulations of the Commercial Registry provide for the registration of EEIGs in Spain. A bill of law introducing the form of the European Economic Interest Grouping into Spanish law was approved on 5 June 1989 by the Congress but was not enacted because the Government dissolved the Parliament in September 1989. A new draft bill is currently under discussion, but has not yet been presented to Parliament. It is unlikely that this bill would affect the existing Regulations relating to registration procedures.
4. COMMENCEMENT DATE: 1 January 1990.
5. DESIGNATED REGISTRY— **address**

   Registration takes place at the Mercantile Registry.

   Registro Mercantil, at the provincial capital where the EEIG has its official address.

   eg Registro Mercantil
   Principe de Vergara 72, bajos
   E-28006 Madrid
   Spain.

   Tel: 34 1 411 39 05 – 34 1 411 44 15
   Fax: 34 1 411 09 05

   —if decentralised— **address**

   eg Registro Mercantil
   Gran Via de les Corts
   Catalanes 184–196
   Barcelona
   Spain.

   Tel: 34 3 332 00 04
   Fax: 34 3 331 94 22

Members of the Groupings must also apply (within one month of the formation contract being approved) to the Delegation de Hacienda (ie tax authorities) in the place where the Grouping has its official address in order to apply for inclusion in the Index of Entities which has been established for corporate tax purposes.

6. DOCUMENTS TO FILED: Formation Agreement duly notarised and translated into Spanish if necessary.
7. FORMS: Application for registration.
   Deposit for publication.
   Application for legislation of statutory books.
8. PROCEDURE: Prior to registration, stamp duty must be paid on the Formation Agreement and EEIG must be registered for taxation purposes.
9. REGISTRATION FEES: Depend on capital.
10. EVIDENCE OF REGISTRATION: Notice of registration will be published in the Boletin Oficial del Registro Mercantil (Official Gazette of the Commercial Registry) and the Official Journal of the European Communities.

WEST GERMANY

EEIG Formation

1. NAME: Europäische wirtschaftliche Interessenvereinigung.
2. ACRONYM: EWIV.
3. NAME OF LAW: Das Gesetz Zwi Ausführung der EWG-Verordnung über die Europäische wirtschaftliche Interessenvereingung (EWIV—Ausfuhrungsgesetz) vom 14 April 1988.
4. COMMENCEMENT DATE: 1 July 1989.
5. DESIGNATED REGISTRY—**address**

   Registered at the local Handelsregister (Commercial Register) in the federal state (Land) in which the EEIG has its official address. Section A of the register is used because EEIGs are similar to Offene Handelsgesellschaften (partnerships) which are registered in that section.

   eg Handelsregister
   Amtsgericht Frankfurt am Main
   Gerichtstrasse 2 (Gebäude B)
   D-6000 Frankfurt 1.

   Tel: 010 49 69 136701
6. DOCUMENTS TO BE FILED: Formation contract.
7. FORMS: Available on request.
8. PROCEDURE: Certain information pursuant to the Regulation must be provided (ie name, location, purpose of business, Managers and duration).
9. REGISTRATION FEES: Varies between local registries—but standard fee is approximately DM600–800.
10. EVIDENCE OF REGISTRATION: Publication of notice in the official gazette of the State in which the EEIG has its official address; the federal official gazette or Bundesanzeiger, and in the Official Journal of the European Communities.

APPENDIX III

Identification of Prospective EEIG Collaborators—Sources

Details of publications listed below are as accurate as possible as at date of publication of this book. Addresses and contact numbers of database hosts, government agencies, or information brokers are also accurate at the time of compilation.
The order of items in this appendix follows Chapter 5.

General Sources

Directories

European Markets: a guide to company and industry information sources
Washington Researchers Publishing Staff
Washington Researchers Publishing
1987, 3rd edn
ISBN 0 934940 86 X.

Macmillan Directory of Business Information Sources
Tudor J D (ed)
Macmillan Publishers Limited
1989, 2nd revised edn
ISBN 0 33348 982 9.

International Directory of Business Information Sources and Services
1986, Europa Publications Limited
ISBN 0 94665 318 6.

Directory of European Associations
Part 1: National, Industrial, Trade and Professional Associations
Anderson Ian Gibson (ed)
CBD Research
1981, 3rd revised edn
ISBN 0 90024 635 9.

Directory of European Associations
Part 2: National, Learned, Scientific and Technical Societies
1984, 3rd revised edn
Adams Robert W (revised by)
CBD Research
ISBN 0 90024 642 1.

Croner's A-Z of Business Information Sources
Croner Publications Ltd
1989, with amendments
ISBN 1 85524 032 7.

Directory of International Sources of Business Information
Ball Sarah (ed)
1989, Pitman
ISBN 0 27303 047 7.

The Source Book
1989, Key Note Publications
ISBN 1 85056 645 3.

ASLIB Directory of Information Sources in the United Kingdom
Vol 1: Science, Technology and Commerce
Vol 2: Social Sciences, Medicine and the Humanities
Ellen M Codlin (ed)
ASLIB Vol 1
1982, 5th edn
ISBN 0 85142 166 0.
ASLIB Vol 2
1984, 5th edn
ISBN 0 85142 184 9.

Lexique UEC
2nd edn
Union Europeenne des Experts Comptables Economiques et Financiers
IdW-Verlag GmbH

Union List of Telephone Directories held by Central London Reference Libraries
1988, 2nd edn
Available from the Senior Information Librarian, London Borough of Tower Hamlets, Bethnal Green Library, Cambridge Heath Road, London E2 OHL.

Disclosure of company documents in the European Community
John Aldis and Jeannot Blanchet (eds)
1989 KPMG.

Databases

ADP Data Services
175 Jackson Plaza
Ann Arbor
Michigan 48106
USA.

CERVED SpA
Via Appia Nuova 696
00179 Rome
Italy.

Data-Star
D-S Marketing Ltd
Plaza Suite
114 Jermyn Street
London
SW1Y 6HJ.

Dialog Information Services Inc
3460 Hillview Avenue
Paolo Alto, CA 94304
USA.

Dun & Bradstreet Limited
Holmers Farm Way
High Wycombe
Bucks
HP12 4UL.

ESA-IRS
CP 64 Via Galileo Galilei
00044 Frascati
Italy.

Harvest Information Services
63 St Martin's Lane
London
WC2N 4JT.

Kompass Online
Windsor Court
East Grinstead House
East Grinstead
West Sussex
RH19 1XA.

MAID Systems Ltd
Maid House,
26 Baker Street,
London
W1M 1DF.

Mead Data Central, Inc
PO Box 933
Dayton, OH 45401
USA.

Orbit Search Service
8000 Westpark Drive, Suite 400
McLean, VA 22102
USA.

Pergamon Financial Data Services
Achilles House
Western Avenue
London
W3 0UA.

Profile Information
Sunbury House
79 Staines Road West
Sunbury-on-Thames
Middlesex
TW16 7AH.

Industry Sources

Directories

Chemistry Industry Yearbook
1984, Chemical Data Services.

Chemical Research Faculties–an international directory
Pollock GL (ed)
1984, American Chemical Society.

Chemfacts
1990, Chemical Intelligence Services, London
ISBN 1 87179 802 7.

Electronic Research Centres
1989, 2nd edn, Longman Group
ISBN 0 58203 604 7.

International Directory of Telecommunications
Roberts Steve (ed); Hay Tony (revised by)
1988, Longman
ISBN 0 58201 890 0.

Databases

Some of the database hosts of these files are shown in brackets after the file name. Please note the list of hosts is not comprehensive.

Financial Times Business Reports (Data-Star, Profile Information).

Insurance Abstracts (Dialog Information Services Inc).

Electronic Publishing Abstracts (Orbit Search Service).

Coffeeline (Dialog).

World Textiles (Dialog).

Artificial Intelligence Online (Dialog, ESA-IRS, Orbit).

European Chemical News (Data-Star).

Predicasts–PTS PROMT (ADP Data Services, Data-Star, Dialog).

Predicasts Newsletter Database (Data-Star, Dialog).

Nexis newsletters.

News Sources

Databases

Financial Times Company Abstracts (Data-Star, Dialog Information Services Inc).

Moody's Corporate News–International (Dialog).

Textline (Reuters).

The Financial Times (Profile–full text : abstracted on many other news databases).

Infomat (Data-Star, Dialog, Pergamon Financial Data Services).

The Financial Times Today (Profile).

Press Cutting Agencies/Alerting Services

HWWA Institut fur Wirstchaftsferschung
Neuer Jungfernstieg 21
2000 Hamburg 36.
Tel: 49 40 3562 260

Informat Ltd
Votec Centre
Hambridge Lane
Newbury
Berks
RG14 5HA.

Premium Business Information Services Ltd
134 Tooley Street
London
SE1 2TU.
Tel: 44 071 403 6033

Newscan
45 Hendham Road
London
SW17 7DH.
Tel: 44 081 767 7007

Press Express
9–10 Great Sutton Street
London
EC1V OBX.
Tel: 44 071 251 9000

Other agencies can be found in the *Advertiser's Annual* published in three volumes by Reed Information Services.

Marketing Information

Directories

Market Research: a guide to British Library Holdings
1988, 5th edn
Barta Eva (ed); Ashpitel S (revised by)
British Library, Science Reference & Information Service
ISBN 0 7123 0745 1.

European Directory of Marketing Information Sources
Shaw Christine (ed)
1987, Euromonitor Publications Ltd
ISBN 0 86338 148 0.

Marketing Surveys Index
Marketing Strategies for Industry
A series of annual loose-leaf volumes updated 10 times per year.
Each annual volume contains details of reports issued in the year in question.

Published data on European industrial markets
1985, Industrial Aids Ltd
ISBN 0 90380 110 8.

Key Note Euroview
Key Note Publications.

Databases

Marketing Surveys Index (Profile Information).

Harvest Marketing Information (Harvest Information Services Limited).

Management and Marketing Abstracts (Pergamon Financial Data Services PFDS).

Advertising and Marketing Intelligence Service Abstracts (Mead Data Central Inc).

Frost & Sullivan Research Report Abstracts (Data-Star).

Euromonitor Market Direction (Profile).

Company Information Sources

Directories

European Company Information : EEC Countries
London Business School Information Service
1989, 3rd revised edn
ISBN 0 95144 010 1.

Duns Europa
Three volumes
1989, Dun & Bradstreet International
ISBN 1 872404 03 3.

Europe's 15000 Largest Companies
1988, ELC International
ISBN 0 948058 36 6.

Major Companies of Europe 1989-90
Three volumes
1989, Graham & Trotman
ISBN 1 853332 95 X.

Country-specific source directories
France 30000
Two volumes
1990, Dun & Bradstreet International
ISBN 0299-4364.

Greens '89 Handbogen om dansk erhversliv
Three volumes
(Danish companies)
1989, Borsens Forlag
ISBN 87 7553 236 0.

Handbuch der Grossunternehmen
(German companies)
1989, Verlag Hoppenstedt.

Financial Directory of Greek Companies
Four volumes
1989, Icap Hellas SA, 24th edn.

Databases

Kompass Europe (Dialog Information Services Inc, Kompass Online).

Europe's Largest Companies (Pergamon Financial Data Services PFDS).

Datastream (Datastream International Ltd).

Disclosure Europe (Disclosure Incorporated).

Diane (Echo Service, Bureau van Dijk/Jordans).

D&B—European Dun's Market Identifiers (Dialog, Data-Star).

Hoppenstedt Germany (Data-Star, Dialog, PFDS, Profile).

ABC Europ (Data-Star) Sp 'Europe'.

Creditreform-Bilanzdatenbank (Data-Star).

Who owns Whom (PFDS).

Company Search Services

Dun & Bradstreet
26-32 Clifton Street
London EC2P 2LY.
Tel: 44 071 377 4377

Jordan & Sons
Jordan House
Brunswick Place
London
N1 6EE.
Tel: 44 071 253 3030

ICC Company Information Services Ltd
16–26 Banner Street
London
EC1Y 8QE.
Tel: 44 071 251 4941

Disclosure UK
London Demand Centre
26-31 Whiskin Street
London EC1R OPB.
Tel: 44 071 278 7848

Credit Rating

Dun & Bradstreet–Dunsprint
Information on this service is available from the address in High Wycombe given under **General Sources**: Databases (p197).

Card Services

Extel European company card service
Extel Financial Ltd
Castle House
37-45 Paul Street
London EC2A 4PB.
Tel: 44 071 253 3400

MIRAC (McCarthy Information Report & Accounts)
McCarthy cards: European service
Both these services are available from:
McCarthy Information Ltd
Manor House
Ash Walk
Warminster
Wilts
BA12 OJP.
Tel: 44 0985 215151

Stockbrokers' Research

Databases

Investext
This online database is available from Dialog or Data-Star.

ICC Stockbroker Research
Available as an online database via ICC Viewdata, Dialog, Data-Star, Pergamon or Profile. ICC also publish a directory to the research they have available.

ARK Information Services
ARK provides copies of European brokers' notes on a subscription or one-off purchase basis. Clients are informed of reports available via a regular catalogue. They can be contacted at:
ARK Information Services
10 Barley Mow Passage
London
W4 4PH.
Tel: 44 081 994 9539

Nexis
This online database service from Mead Data Central, Inc provides access to a wide range of brokers' notes from mainly US stockbrokers.

Management Information Services

The British Institute of Management
Management House
Cottingham Road
Corby
Northants
NN17 1TT.
Tel: 44 0536 204222

Economic and Political Sources

The Europa World Year Book 1990
Two volumes, 1990, Europa Publications Limited.

Oxford Analytica
Further information on the research and consultancy services offered and the Daily Briefs is available from Oxford University.

Frost & Sullivan Political Risk
Information from this source can be accessed as a database on Data-Star.

Reuters Country Reports
Information on political, economic, and social matters can be found on this file available via Reuters Information Services.

Government Agencies

1. *Business Briefing*
   This magazine can be obtained from:
   Business Briefing
   Border House
   High Street
   Farndon
   Chester
   CH3 6PT.
   Tel: 44 0829 270714

2. **Enterprise & Export Initiative**
   Regional Offices
   DTI North East 44 091 232 4722
   DTI North-West 44 061 236 2171
   DTI Yorkshire & Humberside 44 0532 443171
   DTI East Midlands 44 0602 506181
   DTI West Midlands 44 021 631 6181
   DTI South West 44 0272 272666
   DTI South-East 44 071 215 5000 0734 395600 0737 226900
   DTI East 44 0223 461939
   Scottish Office 44 041 248 2855
   Welsh Office 44 0222 825111
   Industrial Development Board for Northern Ireland 44 0232 63244

3. **The Small Firms Service** can be contacted on Freephone 44 088 222 999

4. **Fairs and Promotions**
Fairs and Promotions Branch
Dean Bradley House
Horseferry Road
London
SW1P 2AG.
Tel: 44 071 276 2414

For information on Fairs and Promotions to specific countries contact the numbers below.

West Germany 44 071 276 2539
Belgium, Spain, Portugal, Luxembourg, Finland, Denmark, Iceland, Malta, Norway 44 071 276 2509
Austria, Sweden, Greece, Irish Republic, Switzerland 44 071 276 2506
Netherlands 44 071 276 2507
France, Italy 44 071 276 2503
Eastern Europe 44 071 276 2500

5. **Export Market Information Centre**
1 Victoria Street
London
SW1H OET.
Tel: 44 071 215 5444/5 Fax: 44 071 215 4231

Telephone or fax before your visit to confirm that what you require is available.

6. **Export Opportunities Ltd**
Export House
Wembley Hill Road
Wembley
Middlesex
HA9 8BU.
Tel: 44 081 900 1313 Fax: 44 081 900 1268

7. **Export Marketing Research Scheme**
The Association of British Chambers of Commerce
4 Westwood House
Westwood Business Park
Coventry
CV4 8HS.
Tel: 44 0203 694484

Contracts and Tenders

European Contracts Information Service
Contact Gordon Anderson or Robin Adams at Glasgow University Library, Hillhead Street, Glasgow G12 8AE. Tel: 44 041 330 4283

Tenders Electronic Daily
The TED database is available via Echo Service or Profile Information, both of whose addresses have been given elsewhere.

Dunscontract
Details of this database are available from Dun & Bradstreet in High Wycombe as shown under **General Sources:** *Databases*.

Local Co-operatives

HATRICS
(Hampshire Area Technical Research Industrial Commercial Service)
Hampshire County Library
81 North Walls
Winchester
Hants
SO23 8BY.
Tel: 44 0962 846064

HERTIS
Hatfield Polytechnic Library
College Lane
Hatfield
Herts
AL10 9AD.
Tel: 44 07072 79817

There are many co-operatives in existence and a local public reference library should have details on the one for that particular area.

Information Brokers

Directories

Directory of Information Brokers and Consultants
Crawford MJ (ed) Moody Mary E (ed)
1988, Information Marketmakers
ISBN 0 95114 352 2.

Brokersguide
European Information Market Development Group
Available on the ECHO host system.
Echo Service
177 route d'Esch
1471 Luxembourg.
Tel: 352 488041

Brokers

SVP
12 Argyll Street
London
W1V 1AB.
Tel: 44 071 734 9278

First Contact
224-232 St John Street
London
EC1V 4PH.
Tel: 44 071 490 5519

FTBI
Number One
Southwark Bridge
London
SE1 9HL.

Index